Helen Miller Bailey

Helen Lorraine Miller

Helen Miller Bailey:

The Pioneer Educator and Renaissance Woman Who Shaped Chicano(a) Leaders

Rita Joiner Soza

Rita Joiner Soza

To order additional copies of this book, contact:
www.HelenMillerBaileyBio.com
OR
Xlibris
1-888-795-4274
www.Xlibris.com
Orders@Xlibris.com
695371

CONTENTS

To my teachers
Evelyn and Huston "Bob" Joiner, Alice and Joe Taylor,
Geoff Soza, and Sunny Elizabeth Grean

PREFACE

The Search for Doc Bailey: or Did She Find Me?

Oprah's webcast conversation with Eckhart Tolle had started ten minutes before I could get to my computer. I hadn't known much about Tolle and hadn't read his books, but based on my husband's enthusiastic consumption of *A New Earth*, I wanted to learn more.

As I pulled on my headset, I caught the soft, slow voice in midsentence: "There was not a decision as such, rather an overwhelming feeling that I simply must begin to write." Eckhart Tolle was responding to Oprah's asking why he chose to begin this new project.

I hadn't been prepared for this instantaneous connection. The sensation caused a torrent of tears, as fierce as unexpected. Dr. Tolle was describing exactly how the idea of writing Helen Miller Bailey's biography had emerged—less of a decision—more of a compulsion to take on the work. Many people had asked me why I was even thinking about Doc; I had no valid answer until that moment at my computer. Tolle somehow gave me the permission to continue to pursue this mission regardless of my basically nonexistent knowledge of my former history professor, Helen Miller Bailey, PhD.

My husband walked into my office just at that moment. I quickly wiped my tears away and exited from the Webcast. I felt embarrassed, a bit confused; this was just a little too existential for me, a pragmatic business management instructor. I couldn't explain the emotion I was feeling to myself, let alone to my husband, so I hid my reaction to Dr. Tolle's reply. I pondered the situation for several days thereafter. Was Tolle simply describing inspiration? Somehow that word just didn't seem to capture entirely the actual event of waking up one morning and declaring, "Someone should write a book about Dr. Bailey." Yet in the months ahead, this calling would be explained as the infinite influence of a great teacher reaching out to me. I simply have no other explanation for my strong desire to uncover the story of a teacher who had died some four decades earlier. Unlike Dr. Tolle, I had neither the credentials nor the experience to warrant the audacity to attempt a book; regardless, two years before that Webcast, I had set about researching the very cold trail of a very warm heart.

Luck was on my side, time and time again, once even creating access to one of Helen's book publishers on the very day before the retirement of the keeper of the files on Helen's first textbook. Had I waited twenty-four hours to call Florida State University Press, I would have missed crucial leads in my investigation.

About a year later, I drove up to Los Angeles from San Diego to photograph the home where Helen succumbed to complications from breast cancer treatment. Standing on the sidewalk, I called out my name and stated my purpose to the man behind the screen door, who restrained his huge German shepherd guardian. "Sure, go ahead and take your pictures. I've heard of the professor. It's a good thing you came by today because we're tearing the house down tomorrow!" he shouted above the dog's growls.

Other times when I became frustrated by attempts to verify information, I'd set aside the project, sometimes for months. Invariably when I'd pull out my files and get back into the work of making phone calls or reviewing notes, connections just emerged (when the time was right, I guess).

I researched in spurts of enthusiasm, dragging my dear mom with me to the downtown Los Angeles Central Library and County Hall of Records. We searched through news reports announcing Dr. Bailey's lectures and art exhibits in the 1950s. We grappled with the huge volumes of handwritten documentation of Southern California land transactions in the 1930s. I made endless telephone calls to prospective interview candidates, who usually provided additional leads, some of which I followed up on immediately, some lay dormant for months. In the end, no one ever turned down a chance to reminisce about Helen Miller Bailey; indeed, the result was quite the opposite and their response propelled the work.

On the other hand, guilt was an unexpected emotion which often hindered my work. Shouldn't I be more interested in my own family history? What did my daughter feel as I recounted endless tales of the Bailey's children? While he was always supportive, I never asked my husband if he minded spending money on hotels, long distance phone calls, and out-of-print Latin American textbooks—all to satisfy my curiosity about a woman he had never met.

Thus, I tried to limit/gauge how often the word "Bailey" came up in my everyday conversations, but when I uncovered new evidence or met a new acquaintance of Helen's, my exuberance always won out. Whether feigned or not, but without fail, Evelyn Joiner, Geoff Soza, Sunny Elizabeth Grean, and my best girlfriends from Montebello High School vigorously shared my excitement with each new discovery. Thus, the book is a collaborative work supported by my inner circle, written by all who shared their stories, and through whom many will come to know Helen. The core value we all share with Helen is an understanding that supporting others' potential for greatness is a genuine path to a new earth.

As the first few interviews were completed, the concept of altruism began to develop. I started to understand why telling Helen's story was so important. Indeed, students who claimed Doc had been a formidable force in their lives had emerged from her classroom to achieve illustrious careers in public service. The case can easily be made that several of Helen's students transformed one of the world's greatest cities. In the face of their brilliance, the question to me was even more vivid; why was I the one to write this story?

One of Helen's favorite students and close friend, Richard Avila, explained things to me this way, "Rita, this is just the magic of Helen. Don't you see, she simply found you again." I've come to believe she did. Perhaps the influence of one special teacher dwells in each of us. In Doc Bailey's case, she would likely wish that anyone who reads my account of her life be moved to positive action on others' behalf.

Framing the full canvas of Helen's rich life was a fantastic challenge. Aided by the generosity of her granddaughter, Mary Alice Bailey Welday, who contributed so much, I offer these tales, newspaper accounts, letters, photos, and Helen's own illustrations to all who need reassurance of the goodness in people. Helen's legacy serves as a reminder of the personal power each of us possess to transform lives and shape the future.

Finally, to anyone who has backed away from a project thinking they weren't worthy, I say, "When your inspiration comes, don't deny it. Following your heart can be magical experience!"

FOREWORD

While not new to the Golden State, I am relatively new to El Pueblo de La Reina de Los Angeles, better known as Los Angeles or LA. The majority of my youth and adult life have been spent in San Francisco and the Sacramento region, where I began my service as an educator and then administrator in public higher education. What brings me to LA is my new role as chancellor of the Los Angeles Community College District, the nation's largest and, perhaps, most diverse community college district; it also educates the country's poorest community college students with close to 65 percent of the students living at or near the poverty line.

Like so many students of the Los Angeles region, my parents came to this country with little formal education. Like my own parents, these parents hold on to the dreams and aspirations of their children with a firm grip, all for the hope that the next generation will be better off than the one before. I am a first-generation immigrant, English-language learner from a working class family. Access to higher education and the opportunity that followed was the door to personal discovery and professional exploration, and to renewed hope that was counter to the generations of poverty and isolation that my family and my ancestors unselfishly endured.

As educators, I believe that it is our collective responsibility to purposefully serve our higher education community and, at the same time, to challenge it. We have perhaps the best opportunity to eradicate and overcome social and racial injustice, and to empower the least educated and poorest in our communities. Los Angeles provides a fortuitous opportunity to continue my life's work to serve others through education.

This is where college educator and scholar, artist, and Renaissance woman Helen Miller Bailey comes in. Better known as Doc Bailey or Doc, she too believed in simultaneously serving and challenging education and in empowering others—in this case, the students at East Los Angeles College. Through her activism, art, and scholarship, Doc Bailey influenced a generation of public servants, business professionals, lawyers, educators, and civic activists who attended East. She left an indelible print and transformed the lives of scores of students, several of whom went on to local and national prominence.

Doc Bailey was a trailblazer and was way ahead of her time. Long before the civil rights movement and the educational opportunity programs that followed, Doc Bailey was challenging working-class kids from the east side to know their history, language, and culture. With a missionary zeal, she pushed her students to go to college, to give back to the community, and to serve a greater social purpose. Doc Bailey brought the world to East Los Angeles through her many excursions around the world. She was fully aware that many of her students had never been outside of their neighborhood. She returned with film, photos, and drawings of the many people and cultures that diversify and beautify this world. She provided legitimacy and relevance to the interdisciplinarity of Chicano/Mexican studies, ethnic studies, global studies and women's studies, and exposed her students to being global citizens.

Doc Bailey was a hands-on educator, contributing her own money and convincing others to give money for student scholarships. She also drove students to nearby colleges and universities, making the unfamiliar familiar. In doing so, she bolstered their confidence and self-respect, and as a result, countless first-generation college students entered and graduated from the region's most prestigious institutions.

The results of Doc Bailey's influence and selflessness are truly amazing and inspirational.

I had recent occasion to visit and tour East Los Angeles College, one of the nine colleges within the Los Angeles Community College District. At the center of this east side educational jewel sits the Helen Miller Bailey Library, a beautifully designed, multistory bastion of teaching and learning—a fitting tribute to a pioneering and courageous woman, educator, and philanthropist. I walked through the library thinking of how Doc Bailey would react and respond to the sea of dark-haired, brown-eyed students studying, thoroughly engaged with computers, notes, and books spread out over large tables. I know she is smiling and would be very proud that the seeds she planted many decades ago today are flourishing.

Clearly, the life and legacy of Doc Bailey endures at East Los Angeles College.

Francisco C. Rodriguez, PhD
Chancellor, Los Angeles Community College District

INTRODUCTION
A Seismic Shift on the Eastside

Latin American scholar Helen Miller Bailey provided more than just the academic foundation upon which the Chicano Movement was built in Los Angeles. Upon graduating from university many, who had begun their academic experience with Doc Bailey at East Los Angeles College, went on to develop the new curriculum and teach the previously ignored history. But by all accounts, the pride in their Mexican ancestry was rooted in Doc's lectures, seminal literature, artifact displays, and native dress—all based on years of travel in Latin America and love of the culture.

The examination of her life and impact on her students aims to achieve dual objectives: ignite a passion for service and honor the role of our public community college system for its immeasurable value to a functioning democracy.

At twenty-one Helen Lorraine Miller embarked on what would be a forty-three year teaching career just one year into the Great Depression. This was a challenging time to search for a teaching job, especially for a young woman who just graduated from college. She had earned a master's degree in history from University of California at Berkeley in 1930, supporting herself by waiting tables. The US

Census of that year shows Helen lived in a rooming house run by Mr. and Mrs. Jesse Craig. Other "roomers" included another student, one engineer, four teachers, two druggists, two bankers, and one real estate broker.

So much had changed since she first stepped foot on Cal's campus in 1926. The economy was spiraling down and working women in any field were being urged to give up their jobs to the millions of jobless men. Helen was however offered a one-year teaching contract at Lafayette Junior High (on 12th and Central Avenue), a seismic shift from her parent's dairy farm and the fertile fields of California's Central Valley to the hard clay soil of East Los Angeles. Yet it was here she began her ground-breaking work of introducing generations of underserved students to the world.

A second-year teaching assignment was offered, and it was during that year that Helen met and fell in love with Roosevelt High School physics teacher, Henry Morle Bailey. In addition to their teaching, the couple spent evenings and weekends doing settlement house work from 1931 to 1939 in East Los Angeles. Thus, a circle of love began that would ultimately embrace thousands.

With so many families having lost their incomes during the Great Depression, Los Angeles City School District imposed restrictions against employing married couples so that more families could benefit from teaching jobs; Helen had to quit. With Morle's encouragement, she spent the next two years working on her doctoral degree in history and political science at University of Southern California (USC). In 1935 she was able to return to the classroom at Manual Arts High School with a PhD and the designation of a master teacher from USC's teacher training program. She served as such from 1935 to 1945 at Roosevelt and Manual Arts high schools.

Addressing the great need for higher education among WWII veterans, the California Community College system took on great significance. Though rejected by many gender-biased college presidents, finally, and by competitive examination, Dr. Bailey was hired as the department chair of the social sciences program at East Los Angeles Junior College in 1946. Though race and gender discrimination was prevalent, her high intellect had unlocked the door to higher education teaching. She knew firsthand that entrance into that world for many of her future students would require more courage and the help of mentors.

Helen partnered with a Catholic priest and his parish of Mexican American farm workers in El Monte, California (see chapter 8). Activist priest Father John Coffield, pastor of a migrant encampment, identified high-potential young men and connected them with Dr. Bailey, who enrolled them at the new junior college in East Los Angeles.

The stories these men tell are heartwarming and inspiring. Literally hundreds of Mexican American young men and women have been supported by Dr. Bailey's scholarship funds and moral support. She was the founding advisor/treasurer of the Armando Castro Scholarship Fund in 1955.

When Doc, as she was affectionately known on campus, retired from East Los Angeles College in 1974, colleagues endowed a new scholarship in her name. The fund continues to provide scholarships to deserving high school seniors to smooth their path to their first college semesters.

Dr. Bailey's interest in her Mexican American students' ancestry was evidenced in *Santa Cruz of the Etla Hills*, which she published in 1955 to recount two decades of living with and observing the culture of hillside villagers from Oaxaca, Mexico. One can only imagine the adventurous spirit required to drive from Los Angeles down the newly completed Pan American Highway to Santa Cruz Etla for the first time in 1934. There she worked with locals to build their first school. She helped secure medical services for the community by making monthly tuition payments to a Mexico City nursing school on behalf of a young nursing student from the hill town.

Doc's first international trip was a solo assignment to survey Chinese schools in 1931 on behalf of the YWCA. Later, in biographical notes to one of her textbook publishers, she cited eleven summers spent in Mexico and in Central and South America between 1932 and 1954. While the world focused on the 1936 Berlin Olympic Games, Helen Miller Bailey was bicycling around Hitler's countryside with founders of the American Youth Hostel Association. The following year, Helen travelled to Japan on a special mission studying rural schools. Twenty-five years later, in 1962, she studied rural schools for three months in decolonized Africa. In 1964, she spent a semester in Brazil as a Fulbright scholar.

Excerpts from Doc's handwritten travel diaries have been included to accurately describe the less-than-glamorous conditions of international travel on a teacher's budget. The Baileys headed out on their own (no tours for these adventurers) by car, plane, or ship the day after school let out, often not returning until a day or so before the fall semester began. Doc's classrooms were enriched by her lively observations of conditions abroad, her amateur slide shows and movies, as well as her oil paintings fresh from each summer's expedition to decorate her classroom walls. Fifty short films shot by Helen between 1934 and 1975 have been digitized and made available for viewing on-line by the University of Southern California's Hefner Moving Images Archive *http://uschefnerarchive.com/project/baileyfilms/*.

Known by their grandchildren as Grandma Doc and Grandpa Petie, the loving couple adopted three grown boys and served as long-term foster parents of two others. Rescued from orphanages and other difficult conditions, a focus on education and global travel with their new parents became their new norm. In addition, Helen and Morle provided a home for at least two years for a dozen more young men and shorter term respite for many others. Over the years the Baileys welcomed some ten thousand students into their home for luncheons and dinners.

Upon Helen's retirement in 1974, her former student and close friend Richard Avila offered this tribute, which seems to summon up this work.

> *What can you say about a person who made it possible for thousands of students to obtain a free college education, encouraged an oppressed people to take pride in their ancient heritage, propelled youth into the battle for equal opportunity long before it became fashionable, inspired the study of history as a foundation for contemporary understanding, gracefully accentuated constructive progress while intemperate activists advocated violent remedies, and perennially promoted those honored human values which transcend depression, war, reaction and riots?*
>
> *Many words will be written and spoken about her, and all will be deservedly kind and eloquent. Yet if all of us whom she has known and touched will make of life what she has made—history and truth will record even greater tributes.*
>
> *With love,*
> *Richard Avila*
> [Former California Deputy Attorney General, History Lecturer at East Los Angeles College, and Peace Corps volunteer]

California Mountain Scene, Helen Miller Bailey

CHAPTER ONE
Tarnish on the Golden State

Personal recollections of the author and others are offered to describe the small world and small thinking in which the reader will find Helen Miller Bailey laboring to level the playing field of educational opportunity for East Los Angeles students. Hers was not a statewide initiative or *No Child Left Behind*–type federal program. The Civil Rights Act, Affirmative Action, and the LA Walkouts of 1968 (seeking equal education for all students) came about well after Helen Miller Bailey had immersed herself in Mexican culture and began to transform the hard clay soil of East Los Angeles to fertile ground for studying and preparing for lives of service.

Not-So-Public Facilities

They rode their bikes the three miles to the city swimming pool as many times as their moms would allow them to escape their chores and the summer heat of the San Gabriel Valley. The 1950s offered some advantages—no helicopter parenting meant lots of freedom for adventurous seven- to ten-year-olds (today's baby boomers). Because some could not afford a bike, the smaller kids were perched on handlebars and back fenders—sometimes five on one bike. No one was left behind.

Not until a few years ago did I learn why many of the little bands of Mexican American kids often turned around and headed for home just when they finally arrived at the entrance to the Montebello City Plunge (swimming pool). Assuming they didn't have the nickel entrance fee, the other kids (white kids) never questioned their friends' abrupt return home, for fear of embarrassing their buddies (they too knew days when even a nickel was too much to ask of Mommy or Daddy).

I grew up with the Brick People, so described by Alejandro Morales' 1992 historical novel, on the south side of Montebello, California. During the first half of the twentieth century, their fathers and uncles transformed the hard clay soil into the wrappings of the beautiful buildings of Downtown Los Angeles and Pasadena, as well as the bricks to rebuild San Francisco after the devastating 1906 earthquake. In 1954, two years after the Simons Brickyard closed, *el hoyo*, the giant pit from which the clay had been harvested for fifty years, was ironically filled in with hundreds of thousands of tons of earth from Downtown LA's Bunker Hill (thirty thousand tons per week, reported by the *LA Times*) to carve out space for a new county courthouse.

During my research for this tribute, I read US Ambassador Dr. Julian Nava's autobiography, *My Mexican American Journey*, because he has often written about his inspiring teacher, Doc Bailey. Describing the early years, he shares a story about visiting Mexican American friends from Montebello's south side. Likely he had been there with cousins since earlier in the memoir he had explained that branches of his family lived in *Maravilla* (then a countryside area north of Montebello in East Los Angeles), "which had sprung up like a miracle to house the Mexican immigrant workers of the brickyard" (there were several in the Los Angeles area). In the summer months, he and other beautiful brown-skinned friends were allowed in that very pool only on those days just before it was to be cleaned—if it had just been cleaned, they were turned away.

I was stunned. I called my childhood friend Manuel Lemus, US Marine Corps combat veteran and certified physicians' assistant, who confirmed that, yes, that was the same reason he and other friends couldn't always join our lighter-skinned neighbors in the pool. They had often been cruelly informed to return another day by adults carrying out their own agenda. (We think this practice must have been unknown to Montebello Parks Superintendent Frank Loftis, who Lemus knew to be a very generous spirit.)

As I reflect on those times, I try to focus on the fact that not a single Anglo child in our neighborhood could have ever dreamed up such a vicious reason for our friends' departure from the entrance to the plunge. An innocent heart had to be taught the attitudes and the bias that led to such dreadful behavior on the part of the adults in charge.

But so it was in "mid-Century California." Maria Fleming's article, "A Tale of Two Schools," published by the Southern Poverty Law Center, reports that Mexican Americans in California and all over the Southwest were also excluded from "Whites Only" theaters, parks, restaurants, and even barbershops in the early 1900s.

Separate but Unequal Schools

In some ways we were better off than kids who grew up in the heart of East Los Angeles; our neighborhood had a little more land to run around in, but we also knew classmates whose homes had dirt floors and those who came to school in raggedy clothes.

When I started Greenwood Elementary in 1955, it was *integrated*. It may seem an exaggeration to use such a term to describe California schools that allowed Mexican Americans to learn alongside their Anglo neighbors, but in years prior, many of my neighbors would have been forced to attend their own hovel of a school nearer Simons Brickyard.

In 1947 separate (and unequal) schools were the norm until two Mexican American families sued an Orange County school district that had only allowed their fair-skinned children to attend the better-equipped white school. Their darker brothers and sisters were sent away. The *Mendez v. Westminster* case and others that followed lead to the reversal of *Plessy v. Ferguson*, the legal decision that had required supposed separate but equal schools to become the norm. In 1954, Chief Justice Earl Warren (former California governor) penned the Supreme Court's decision that ended legal racial segregation of schools.

This Land Is Your Land, This Land Is My Land . . . Which Is It?

The history of Mexicans living in California from the 1930s through the 1950s is a tale of fickle policies, which deported millions back to Mexico only to have other Mexicans be encouraged to migrate when the country needed cheap labor. Two waves of repatriations to Mexico from the United States took place in this period.

Cal State University Los Angeles history professor Dr. Francisco E. Balderrama has reported that of the 1.2 million people of Mexican ancestry who were deported, four hundred thousand were from California and approximately 65 percent overall were US-born. Harsh consequences existed for many who were missed in the community raids. For a description of Dr. Nava's own near deportation and the policy's devastating impact on his family, see chapter 15).

Not only were Mexican and Mexican American families subject to random deportations, they were also restricted from living in many California cities. Thus you find Dr. and Mr. Bailey and many other professionals working at All Nations Settlement House in the early 1930s providing all number of services to immigrant families. Because these restrictions eased after WWII, I hadn't personally been aware of such conditions. At fifteen, I started working for a successful Mexican American family, who owned a chain of dry cleaners in the San Gabriel Valley but lived miles away near the Los Angeles/Orange County border. I still remember the stinging response to my questioning why the family didn't move closer to their businesses. I learned they simply remained loyal to the town that had accepted their hardworking parents years before, despite their financial and legal freedom to move as they wished in the late sixties.

No Ivory Towers, Just Tin Walls

The less overt and perhaps more insidious brand of prejudice persisted in the public schools. "Educational leaders of those post–WWII days, all Anglos, were not attuned to the problems of minority groups," Dr. Bailey wrote in a history of East Los Angeles College

(ELAC), "While they were pleased to be offering all veterans college education on the GI Bill," there was an undercurrent of opposition in 1945 to accommodating a community college on the grounds of Garfield High School of *Stand and Deliver* fame. "Why build a college on the Eastside? Those people won't know what to do with a college," expresses the attitude held by many Anglo and Westside Los Angelenos. Not surprisingly, the first students quickly nicknamed the new institution East, almost as if daring to utter the words *college* and *East Los Angeles* in the same phrase might jinx the school's very existence.

Helen apologized in her 85-page account of the college's beginnings for the "little recognition of the large local Spanish-speaking population in the columns (of the college newspaper). Such recognition just wasn't there, except as it listed, in increasingly large numbers, Spanish last names among award winners, student leaders, and graduates. The consciousness that the Spanish-last name students needed recognition of their own culture only began to take hold in the 1960s."

Doc explained that Dr. Roscoe Ingalls, who had helped found Garfield High School in 1925 and had years later been appointed president of Los Angeles City College, promised local newspaper owner Arthur Baum he would return to the Eastside where these two stronger forces for good would realize their dream of a college in East Los Angeles. "During his war time years at City College he [Ingalls] lost both of his sons," Dr. Bailey reported, "thus in one sense the junior college was a memorial to Chandler and Hugh Ingalls, those young sons."

The new college graduated its first three students in June 1946. UCLA's Dean of the School of Education spoke to the audience of about three hundred on "the pioneer spirit." By the spring of 1947, one thousand one hundred students were enrolled and a bond issue passed providing funds to purchase the farmland along Brooklyn Avenue, Cesar Chavez Boulevard today; the eighty-two acres had been planted in barley with cattle pastures framing the northern hillside border of the property.

Dr. Nava described how those first students, his classmates, slugged through the mud from one temporary building to another to eagerly attend college classes. These were Quonset huts—eight in total—donated from what had been the wartime Santa Ana Army Air Base training center. Unlike the ivory towers of Harvard where Nava later earned his doctoral degree, no ivy grew on the tin walls of these buildings.

In an interview for Smithsonian Archives of American Art in 1992, actor and avid art collector Vincent Price (1911-1993) described his own first encounter with the college in 1948 (after years of disappointment with the visual art community of West LA and Beverly Hills).

> *My involvement with East Los Angeles is because it couldn't happen there [broken promises]. It's much too honest a neighborhood. It is completely isolated from this world over here [Beverly Hills]. It's completely different. I was invited to come and talk to this college, which was about five Quonset huts on a mudflat, by a woman named Judith Miller [first art department chair]. And she wanted me to talk about the aesthetic responsibility of the citizen. That's a pretty classy title. Well, it fascinated me since the aesthetic responsibility of Quonset huts on a mudflat was not very high. But I went, and I fell in love with it, fell in love with the whole Latino community...this was where I*

decided to put my energy, and to do it without any way
identifying myself with it. Because I was accused here of
using the arts as an entrée to a world that I didn't want
to be in anyway. People sort of said, 'He's an art snob.'
It's very difficult for me to talk about it. But that's why
forty-five years ago I started this collection in East Los
Angeles."

Because of the generosity of Mary and Vincent Price and the museum he supported on ELAC's campus, we now have access to the films Helen shot around the world from 1934 to 1975. Some 50 films were donated to the Vincent Price Museum upon her passing and years later passed on to USC's Hefner Moving Images Archive - *http://uschefnerarchive.com/project/baileyfilms/.*

The infrastructure at East had improved a good deal by 1961 when Richard Alatorre graduated from Garfield High School. In a short fifteen years the junior college, as they were all called then, had become the recognized transitional institution for high school grads seeking guaranteed entry to four-year California universities. But those who qualified to enter the universities directly were all eligible for admittance, right?

While many of his friends and family started college at ELAC, Richard had the grades and the ambition to go straight to California State University Los Angeles (CSULA). His problem was his counselor, "No no no. Let's get you signed up at junior college first."

You see, nearing graduation my counselors refused
to forward my application to Cal State. They decided I
should attend (what was then called) junior college first,
before attempting a four-year school, explaining their

refusal was strictly "for my own good." What helped me
was my experience in student government. I hadn't spent
all those semesters working on behalf of the student body
at Garfield to allow someone else to control my future.
I took my qualifying grades and my advisors' refusals
directly to the principal. Cal State may not accept me—I
can live with that. But, I cannot accept someone stopping
me from trying.

Determined Alatorre marched through the application process on his own and went on to graduate from CSULA and earn a master's degree from University of Southern California (USC). In his 1989 *Los Angeles Times* article, reporter Bill Boyarsky proclaimed Richard Alatorre to be "the most influential Latino politician in California." (See chapter 12 to learn about Alatorre's connection to Dr. Bailey.)

Another important California political figure Lou Moret recalled his many conversations with Doc Bailey at ELAC and the second chance the school represented:

I was a late starter and was 25 when I returned to
ELAC (after being kicked out earlier.) I had three kids, a
wife and we were buying our first house.

Dr. Bailey was very helpful and encouraging. She was
my teacher and a really giving, caring woman. She really
wanted especially Mexican Americans to reach their full
potential since we didn't get too many breaks in those
days. She was in the forefront of social activism.

I graduated from ELAC in 1969 and went on to
Whittier College. Upon graduation I ran Richard
Alatorri's campaign and became his chief of staff and

that started a career in politics and public service. I ran
Art Torres' campaign for state senator. I believe I was
the first Latino to achieve a Presidential appointment. In
1977 President Carter appointed me first Director of the
Office of Minority Economic Impact in the Department
of Energy.

Around that same time, a young graduate of USC was interviewing for his first teaching job. Today a trustee of the iconic Los Angeles institution, Frank Cruz, described the Los Angeles City Schools recruiter's disbelief when he turned down teaching opportunities at well-funded Westside schools in favor of high schools on the Eastside, where his mentor Helen Miller Bailey had begun her teaching career, "He just couldn't believe I wanted to return to the barrio. He didn't understand what that college degree meant and how we had been inspired to service by professors like Doc Bailey."

State-Supported Indignities

In his second career as the first Latino television news anchor in Los Angeles, Frank Cruz reported daily on one of the most tragic results of racial prejudice in California's history, which was fostered by the faulty science of eugenics. (Read more about Cruz' relationship with Helen and his fascinating career in chapter 13.)

Even with the knowledge that the Holocaust was the horrific result of Eugenicists' theories, a global belief persisted that less-robust breeds should be discouraged from tainting the human race. Indeed, California led the way in the nearly nationwide practice of unwanted sterilization of indigents, infirm, criminals, and nonwhites being treated in state hospitals.

This practice was particularly brutal and came to light at Los Angeles County General Hospital in East Los Angeles in 1972. Non-English-speaking maternity ward patients in the midst of labor were offered tubal ligations, which they gratefully accepted although they had no idea what the words meant. Imagine the humiliation of having unwittingly agreed to sterilization in a matriarchal culture. Some of the victims Cruz interviewed never confessed the procedure to their family members. Read more about the role of Helen Miller Bailey's students in the repeal of California's involuntary sterilization law in chapter 14.

Such a lack of human dignity existed even within families from East Los Angeles, wherein there is an inevitable blend of Mexicans, Russians, Jews, Armenians, and Japanese. For example, in the early 1980s, I married a man whose ancestors founded Tucson, Arizona. Though his Russian mother and Mexican American father, who had met and married in the Boyle Heights section of East LA, had divorced in 1955, my husband still held the belief that Soza was a Portuguese surname. At the time, "wetback" and "dirty Mexican" were terms commonly used to describe people like my husband's paternal family who had settled in the Southwest long before any Anglo exploration of the region.

Indeed, the institutional use of such racial slurs as late as the 1960s is evidenced by the Immigration and Naturalization Service's own "Operation Wetback" designed to strengthen borders and conduct targeted deportations. In this racially charged environment his mom had decided he should be known as one-half Russian and one-half Portuguese, instead of Mexican. Not until age thirty-seven did my husband learn the truth. Today we are all immensely proud of his Mexican heritage and the Soza Family Museum in downtown Tucson.

From the Farm to a Place at the Table

In 2005 I learned that my old college professor Doc Bailey had operated an underground railroad of sorts back in the mid-1940s. I shouldn't have been shocked that Mexican Americans living with their migrant farm worker parents were not allowed to enroll at East Los Angeles College when it first opened.

I shouldn't have been shocked, and I was. The Chicano Movement was rooted in that farmland on Brooklyn Avenue. Chicanos not allowed was a paradox I couldn't wrap my mind around. Chapter 7 offers stories of Helen's collaboration with the parish priest from the pickers' camps and the students' subsequent contributions to California society.

In addition to securing entrance to a college education for generations of marginalized East Los Angelenos, Doc Bailey developed genuine relationships with her students. Former Mexican American Legal Defense Fund (MALDEF) CEO and General Counsel Antonia Hernandez explains that academic encouragement for a young female Mexican American student was very rare even in the late sixties when she attended ELAC. Hernandez recollects that throughout her many years of schooling, Helen (and one high school math teacher) was the only teacher who ever expressed an authentic interest in her as an individual. The two women remained friends until Helen's death.

Helen's was a one-woman, ground-floor effort—quite literally. In fact, legend has it that she could be seen early in the morning out in the college parking lot adjacent to the busy boulevard picking up cigarettes butts and any other debris, lest morning commuters gain any support for the idea that her students were unworthy of the grand institution she was helping to build.

Though it's been decades since her death, anyone who travels along Cesar Chavez Boulevard cannot miss the impressive East Los Angeles College campus and its state-of-the-art Helen Miller Bailey Library, rededicated in 2012 after renovations nearly doubled its capacity.

Helen Miller Bailey Library
East Los Angeles College, Monterey Park, California

California countryside by Helen Miller Bailey

CHAPTER TWO

A Modesto Termite Flies South to Los Angeles

Social Sciences Department Chair Helen Miller Bailey hired Dr. Phyllis Woodworth to teach psychology at East Los Angeles College (ELAC) in the mid-1950s when it was still difficult for a woman to land a professorship, even at a "junior" college. Phyllis proved to be a good choice. She ended her own teaching career as ELAC's social sciences department chair, a role she had accepted upon Helen's retirement in 1974.

When contacted for an interview, Phyllis Woodworth didn't think she had much concrete information to contribute to the research about her predecessor. Phyllis proved to be incorrect, on that point.

Soon after apologizing for her poor memory, Dr. Woodworth recalled Helen's retirement dinner, which had been attended by local politicians, former students, community leaders, family, and teaching colleagues. The five hundred guests gathered in an elegant ballroom, (for Eastside standards), of the Luminarias restaurant, just one mile from East Los Angeles College atop a hill overlooking Interstate 10, Cal State University Los Angeles, and Los Angeles County General Hospital (now University of Southern California Medical Center.) Phyllis agreed with the Bailey grandchildren, distinguished guests, and press accounts that the event was a fitting tribute to Helen's forty-three-year teaching career. Reflections on the party stimulated Phyllis's memories of working with Helen:

Although I wasn't close to her personally, I liked Helen and admired her as a department chair. You see, women in higher education faced tremendous discrimination in those days. I do think Helen was particularly proud of the female faculty she hired at East Los Angeles College in the 1950s because of our courage and support of each other.

When reviewing letters presented to Helen at the Luminarias event, one stood out in support of Phyllis's claim. Elisabeth C. Condon thanked Helen for hiring her daughter Mary in 1955, after all the young PhD's job applications had been rejected by others. Mrs. Condon explained,

> At that time Dr. Bailey proved that she was years ahead of civil rights (legislation) which protects the rights of equality as to sex. Dr. Condon had taken the examinations for a college position in the city school system for several years and following each test she would receive a letter explaining that although her score was very high the colleges were not hiring women. Finally she was placed on the list and Dr. Bailey did not discriminate against her either as to sex or her religion (Catholic).

Teaching under Dr. Bailey was a joy for Mary. While my daughter was teaching at ELAC each year Dr. Bailey encouraged (her) to have a member of the social work profession present a program on the opportunities for a professional social worker, particularly Spanish speaking Mexican Americans.

Mary Condon was hired away from ELAC in 1963 by the University of Santa Clara. When she died in 1971 at just fifty-five, her colleagues endowed the Dr. Mary Condon Memorial Book Fund for deserving students.

Not only did Phyllis provide insight into the gender discrimination women in higher education endured during the first half of the twentieth century, she also offered some special knowledge that not even Bailey family members had known, "Helen was very bright, a Terman Kid you know." "No, I don't know. What is a Terman Kid?" I was happy to be on the phone so Phyllis couldn't see the confused look on my face. "Dr. Terman—from Stanford—the Stanford-Binet IQ test Terman!" she grunted, clearly annoyed. Silence on my end of the line apparently signaled her teaching skills to surface, "Helen was a very bright child who was selected, along with 1,500 other California children with IQ scores above 135, to participate in one of the largest longitudinal studies ever undertaken. You'll need to read about Professor Terman's study if you want to have a better understanding of who Helen was."

Subsequent interviews always revealed some unknown characteristic of Dr. Bailey, whose complexity prompts the recast modifier "Renaissance woman" —the great beauty, avid painter, influential teacher, world traveler, author, social activist, super mom—now *bona fide* genius must be added to the image.

Having often lectured to civic groups regarding her world travels, exhibiting her paintings, and participating in several statewide educational reform task forces, Helen Miller Bailey wasn't shy about her accomplishments; however, she did not publicize her participation in Dr. Terman's study. Indeed Phyllis Woodworth was one of the very few contemporaries with whom Helen spoke of Terman.

While I can imagine how the topic might come up among the two social science professors, I suggest, with some confidence, that given Helen's lifelong devotion to educating the underprivileged, she may have been philosophically opposed to what many believe motivated Terman's research: differentiating intellectual capacity among racial and ethnic groups.

Identifying the Brightest California Has to Offer

During 1910, the year of his appointment to Stanford University's Department of Education, the psychology professor would expand upon and develop age differentiations to improve the Binet-Simon intelligence scale. Terman's version, the Stanford-Binet intelligence quotient (IQ), which he ardently promoted, gained widespread use in American schools. Dr. Terman's intent was to identify and nurture the most gifted individuals from a young age, to endow society with a continuous flow of talented future leaders.

Thus, Terman's motivation was in direct contrast to that of French educators Alfred Binet and Theodore Simon, who developed the original version of the assessment in 1905 to identify struggling students in order to ensure them additional support from the French educational system. Given Helen's life work it seems reasonable to presume she would have been more aligned with Binet's mission.

Indeed, his detractors say Terman endeavored to prove the superiority of individuals with IQs over 135 in hopes of engineering a meritocracy run by those he believed most qualified to lead. Mitchell Leslie reports in July/August 2000 *Stanford Magazine*:

> *The author of the path breaking Genetic Study of Genius was a proponent of eugenics, a social movement aiming to improve the human "breed" by perpetuating certain allegedly inherited traits and eliminating others. A popular science in America and Europe prior to WWII (with dreadful consequence in Nazi Germany), eugenics was viewed by many well-to-do whites as a solution to the reproduction of the "unfit," which included the frail, emotionally unstable, and "shiftless." Thirty-three states, including California, passed measures requiring sterilization of the feebleminded. As a result, more than sixty thousand men and women in mental and other institutions were sterilized, most against their will. This practice continued in the United States well into the 1970s, albeit with the knowledge of the Nazis' early 1940s mass sterilization programs.*

Early to Ripe, Early to Rot

Others believe Dr. Terman's was a more personal quest since he could have been labeled a genius himself. He reportedly regretted his lack of special promotion, and rather endured the outright humiliation, he and similar children felt from the school system of their time. "Early to ripe, early to rot" paraphrased the folklore surrounding the often precocious youngsters of high intellect at the turn of the twentieth century.

Terman and his successors would later debunk the then-popular notion that very smart children were physically weak and singular in their abilities, thus socially inferior individuals. Difficult to imagine today, but adjectives such as "bright" and "gifted" were not used to describe smart children, until Terman took up their banner.

So Terman set out to prove his hypothesis, which Stanford science writer Joel N. Shurkin describes in his book, *Terman's Kids: the Groundbreaking Study of How the Gifted Grow Up*, as the "belief that the future of the United States lay with discovering and nurturing its brightest children. He believed that intelligence was inherited, that parents passed genius on to their children, and that not enough of the very bright children were being produced."

By 1928 Terman had assembled 1,528 California youngsters whose Stanford-Binet scores indicated genius. These children became the subjects of a monumental study, which would last over fifty years, continued by Stanford psychology professors Robert and Pauline Sears long after Terman's death in 1956. After the Sears retired from Stanford, and until 2009, Professor Albert Hastorf was the keeper of the study's annual survey results.

Terman's Hands-On Approach Breaches Scientific Protocol

In addition to Terman's handpicked subjects from Los Angeles, San Francisco, and the East Bay neighborhoods, hundreds of participants were recommended by school principals and volunteer testers. Exactly how Modesto, California, resident Helen Lorraine Miller became a participant is not known.

Scientific criticism of the results of Terman's work arose not only from his motivational biases but later from his involvement in subject outcomes. These were his kids . . . his Termites. He helped ensure their opportunities by writing letters of recommendation and more.

For example, *Stanford Magazine* reports in the case of Termite Jess Oppenheimer, creator and head writer of the iconic television sitcom *I Love Lucy,* Terman arranged Oppenheimer's transfer to Stanford from the University of San Francisco despite the future playwright's less than stellar academic record.

A glimpse at how Helen might have similarly benefitted may have been revealed in a brief autobiographical account, "one day I woke up at seventeen and found myself off our Modesto dairy farm and on the Berkeley campus, not knowing exactly how or why I had arrived." Whether or not Terman intervened on Helen's behalf, this Termite did graduate at twenty years old with a master's degree in history from University of California at Berkeley in 1930. The following year she accepted a teaching assignment in the barrios of East Los Angeles where she flourished as an educator, Latin America scholar, and textbook author.

Jobs weren't easy to come by in that first year of the Great Depression. Had Terman helped out again, or were teaching assignments in poor, inner city, underserved areas not sought after by many, making such a post easier to secure, or was Helen simply drawn to such service?

Pauline Sears Compares Career Women with Other Female Respondents

Pauline Sears, who had become a professor at Stanford, after earning her PhD in psychology from Yale in 1939, took on the analysis of the ongoing participant surveys after Terman's death. Sears contrasted the responses from women like Helen and herself, who had careers (still not the norm until the early-1970s) with those who did not work outside the home.

Sears reported that an extraordinary 67 percent of the 430 female participants earned bachelor's degrees, compared to 8 percent (typical for the age group at that time). A *San Francisco Chronicle* interview quotes Sears:

> *Gifted women made it even if they only had a high school education. I lay this to their intelligence. They worked their way up to good jobs . . . These women were ahead of their time. They had fewer children. With their intelligence level they had the capacity to solve any problems that presented themselves. It should be noted that, while many of those listed as homemakers now say they wished they had worked, none of the workers said the same about being homemakers.*

An observer of the Bailey home might have guessed Doc would have answered those survey questions similarly. While the Bailey house was filled with young people, Dr. Bailey wasn't involved in much housework. The last of the Bailey housekeepers (inheritor of Helen's textbook royalties), Carlotta Saenz, maintained the household while male students living with the Baileys often helped with Mr.

Bailey, who was wheelchair-bound from 1955. In addition to her teaching classes, fighting for social causes, painting, and planning family travels, Helen religiously swam and read the newspaper every day. Time for domestic chores was limited or simply shrugged off.

Terman's study of geniuses showed a "very significant difference" between those women who had chosen to become "income earners" and those who had chosen to be homemakers. Of the former, 79 percent expressed high satisfaction with their lives, compared to 62 percent of the homemakers. Sears is quoted in a 1975 *New York Times*' article, "Those [women] without children were considerably more satisfied with their work pattern than were those with children." How satisfied was Helen with her life? Did she report herself as a woman with or without children? Did she count the three adopted boys or the couple dozen or so who shared her home over the years?

Clearly, this income earner was driven to achieve—produce textbooks, paintings, and college graduates. Even after her retirement and cancer diagnosis, she was hired by the City of Montebello, California, to write that town's history. About that same time she also completed an eighty-five-page history of East Los Angeles College. Had she been planning other projects? We imagine so, even though Helen did spend the last year of her husband's life at home nursing him and the following year losing her own battle with the brutal cancer treatment of the day.

Folder 37, Box 24—Lost

Joel Shurken was very supportive during phone conversations in 2005 and 2009. Professor Shurken was the first to be allowed in the sanctuary of the School of Psychology at Stanford University where the confidential files of over 1,500 California geniuses are housed, supposedly. He explained that although Helen was not one of the specific Termites he had profiled for his book, he could describe the room in which he conducted his research at Stanford. Professor Shurken explained that the file boxes which contained the survey information for each participant were held under the tightest controls, in accordance with the initial participant agreements assuring anonymity. Most importantly, he provided the contact who might confirm Helen's participation in Terman's study.

I would love to believe that Helen had indicated a great deal of satisfaction with her life. Unfortunately, that will likely never be known. While Professor Emeritus Hastorf was able to confirm that Helen was indeed a Termite, his staff was unable to locate her file. Fifty years of responses to questions about Dr. Bailey's satisfaction levels with her career, her love life, her views on politics and religion—all lost—the content of box 24, folder 37—all lost.

As of this writing Helen's surviving family members remain devastated on this account. (See Appendix A.)

The summary data does show however that Helen was among the two-thirds of Termites who earned a bachelor's degree (ten times the national rate for the time) and one of the ninety-seven PhDs in the study. The last survey Helen would have participated in was administered in 1972 by Professor Sears who reported results in *People* magazine.

> *When these women answered the questionnaire, in 1972, they were approaching retirement age [Helen was 63 then]. I identified with them since I was about to retire from Stanford University myself. They were asked to look back and see what they had done with their lives, and their answers interested me. Because of my background, for*

example, I hoped we would find that professional careers
were associated with satisfaction—and we did.

Was Helen included in that group? The answer may never be known unless some day box 24, folder 37 is located.

How participation in Terman's study influenced Helen's life is really conjecture. The Baileys legally adopted three at-risk boys who were not reported to possess superior intelligence. While many of the students Helen mentored and welcomed into her home (as they struggled financially to complete a college education) could be described as quite bright, no evidence of selection based on any criteria other than need brought these young people into the embrace of Helen and Morle Bailey. While Helen helped several people identify their leadership capabilities, too much evidence exists to support any thought that she would have aligned herself in any way with the more sinister notions that may have guided Terman's work.

Perhaps Helen shared her Termite status with Phyllis Woodard as more of a point of shared academic curiosity. Perhaps her lack of sympathy with Terman's suspected motivation is why she rarely mentioned her participation in the study to other friends or family (at least not to those interviewed for this account). Perhaps Helen herself removed her confidential responses from the "vault" in the Stanford Psychology Department in an effort to disassociate herself from Terman. Perhaps there is no record of the last person to have been allowed to view her records, because subjects themselves were permitted to enter the files. So many unknowns. . .

The irony is not lost on the story revealed in chapter 14, which describes how five of Dr. Bailey's devoted students were instrumental in the repeal of a California eugenics-inspired law sanctioning involuntary sterilization of inmates and patients in State institutions.

Helen Lorraine Miller

Chinese Countryside, Helen Miller Bailey

CHAPTER THREE

Helen's Letter Home: 1931 Steamship to China

After her graduation in 1930 from University of California at Berkley, Helen Lorraine Miller was awarded a one-year teaching assignment in Los Angeles. The following summer she travelled by steamship throughout Asia at the request of the YWCA to report on the condition of Chinese schools. Her sponsors could not have known they were actually sending the twenty-one-year-old on a very treacherous journey.

According to National Oceanic and Atmospheric Administration (NOAA) climatologists, China suffered massive flooding caused by prior years of drought, followed by a heavy winter's snowfall and spring melt which combined with heavy rains in July and August of 1931. An estimated 4 million people "perished from the greatest disaster of the twentieth century due to disease, starvation or drowning." In his 2002 *Engineering the State: The Huai River and Reconstruction in Nationalist China 1927-1937*, David Pietz describes conditions on August 25, 1931 when Grand Canal dikes were washed away in the middle of the night and two hundred thousand people drowned in their beds.

With no way of foreseeing the massive devastation the country was about to experience during her stay, Helen voices her frustration with the storm conditions in a letter home:

> *S. S. Tjikarang* (letterhead)
> *July 26, 1931, Sunday*
> *Yellow Sea*
>
> *Dear Everybody:*
> *This is all the Honest to God Truth—with no exaggerations nor anything—just exactly like it happened and nobody to thank but these blessed Dutchmen and that pink voile dress.*
> *Well, I wrote you on the Shinyo Marce en route to Shanghai that last night there was a sort of little typhoon, electric storm and endless cloudbursts of rain. We pulled into Shanghai a half day late—The Chinese doctor (C. L. Lung) we had met on the Asama was waiting for us in the pouring rain and got us quickly through customs—he had made reservations for us at the Astor House Hotel, where we had a fine dinner and sat around and chatted with a bunch of Honolulu teachers in the evening while the storm raged.*
> *I was wakened at 10:00 the next morning by the terrible news that all the trains to Peking had been washed*

out. We were inconsolable—as that meant staying in Shanghai where there is little to see for two weeks till the Asama came back. We tore over to the China Travel Office. Although Miss Gray (business manager) stormed and argued, the river steamers cannot go because of the storm—If there was a coast steamer we could get to Lsing Loa. But the only steamer going has a waiting list of more than 100 and they cannot book any more on the train from Lsing Loa to Peking because it is crowded for days ahead. There is absolutely nothing to do but stay in Shanghai.

Dr. Lung called for the five of us at 8:00 the next morning and took us to the China Travel Bureau, which arranges all the trips to Peking, where we had paid our money and made our reservations on the special first class express leaving for a 48 hour run to Peking Sunday a.m. Then we went to the government office to get Chinese Visas which took hours. It was a quarter to 12:00 when we got out but as it had stopped raining the others wanted to shop.

So I left them with Dr. Lung and went alone by rickshaw to find the Java Steamship office (I wrote you about the card and introduction Mr. Bos and Mr. Offenberg had given me, didn't I?) There I met a bespectacled droll young Mr. Johann Louis Mark Frederiks, who translated my famous card to say "a charming young lady" (I'm afraid I never will find out just what it did say, as Mr. Frederiks kept it.) Anyway, he took me to lunch at the "Palace Hotel" (more orange squash—to keep up with his sparkling Burgundy, which I tried and was disappointed). I had by this time a very bad cold which I took back to my hotel and doctored and put to bed to the accompaniment of a rereading of your precious letters.

After we have given up a chance to go to Manila, after I have broken the time of my life in Hong Kong right in two in order to see Peking all five us of want to cry. The others go back to the hotel and do it. But I console myself by going to lunch with Mr. Fredericks. Mr. Lee has arranged us a Chinese dinner in the native city. The three of us go to quite a beautiful (but dirty) place and have a repast two hours long—preserves, eggs, birds nest soup, fried shrimp, shark's fins, duck stew, noodles, bean cakes, tea, rice, Chinese wine (no orange squash available!) all with beautiful dishes and carved ivory chop sticks. I voice my anguish over the Peking failure a couple of times and then return to Astor House.

Mr. Fredericks called at 6:00 and took me to the French Club, a famous cabaret, where we met his Norwegian chum and a pretty English girl for dinner and dancing (in the pink voile dress). At 9:00, a young Chinese accountant from the Java S. S. office arrived with the best, reserved tickets at the most exclusive Chinese theatre in Shanghai, so the four of us rushed off in a Norwegian car.

The Chinese theatre owner, Mr. Lee, was so honored to have us he introduced us to all the Chinese actors as "my dear friends." The seats were in a sort of box with embroidered cushions and little tile tables from which we drank tea and ate melon seeds and peanuts and bean cakes while we watched at very close range one of the most entertaining shows I've seen—beautiful costumes, an elaborate story explained to us by Mr. Lee step by step.

Some long winter evening when I have more time and feel better I'll explain it all to you. We left when the show was half finished at about 12:00 and returned to the hotel in the worst storm I'd seen yet.

Back at the travel office where Mr. Frederiks and Mr. Lee have much pull. Yes, yes, yes they can get us train reservations from Lsing Loa (anything to please the Dutch S. S. Co.) but alas, there is no steamer up the coast to Lsing Loa—nothing can be done. We go sadly back to the Java S. S. office—Now just after lunch, the Java freighter Tjikarang, loaded with sugar has pulled into Shanghai from Hong Kong for a couple of hours.

The captain breezes into the office. Says he, "I hear Offenberg and the Junior Consul found a pretty little girl in Hong Kong and sent her up here. What became of her?" says the jolly passenger agent, to whom I had voiced my troubles that morning, "Oh, she's out with Fredericks, all upset over the railroad being out to Peking." Says the captain, "I'll drop her at Tsing Lao on the way to Dalian. I have room for eight more passengers."

So, when Frederiks and I trooped disconsolately back through the rain, here was a steamer all ready and waiting to take me to Lsing Loa. I rushed to the hotel for Miss Gray, we rushed to the China Travel office for our train tickets to be changed, rushed to the Java office for these five special tickets on the Tjikarang, rushed to the hotel and packed, and the five of us get on Mr. Frederik's launch and go out to the Tjikarang in the harbor (still pouring rain) in time for it to pull out at 5:30. The other three, bring rushed through all this, had no idea where we were going or why until we got on the freighter.

The passenger accommodations, though very seldom used, are really very nice. Miss Gray and I ate with the captain, the ship's doctor and the first engineer. The other three (Miss Thoren, Miss Padrisk, Miss Berry) ate with the second and third officer. We all played Michigan after dinner in the tiny little lounge. We will be in Lsing Lao tomorrow noon and in Peking Tuesday. It will cost us less than the train, the food is better and these Dutchmen are fine—all speak English. But my cold is terrible—I am propped up in bed writing but shall get up for lunch.

Dr. Lung was going to take the other four through the native city Saturday night and I was going to a dance with Mr. Fredericks—But now it's Peking or bust! I have come up with a bang in Miss Gray's estimation because of my coup d'etat and my "private steamer." Will write from Peking.

Love to all,
Helen

A few days later July 31, 1931, Helen writes from the North China Union Language School, Peking, China:

I hope you will get this before I get home. We are in San Francisco on August 26. I don't know what time of day, but that is 3 weeks from next Wednesday. It'll probably be just the wrong reason for you to meet the boat, though I'm afraid no one else will be there . . . I shall call Los Angeles right away to ask about the jobs. If there is one already for me I'll go right to Modesto, stay there till Friday and arrive in LA Saturday, August 29 to look up my new job. If there isn't a job yet, I'll only stay with you Wednesday night. I'll have to be in Berkeley only long enough to find Miss Mary Ross and give her some crystals I bought her. I am not at all anxious to go back to LA, but, since my vacation is more than half over, I am quite distinctly worried about next year. But, it's no use thinking about it—especially since I am still having such a beautiful time.

Helen Lorraine Miller aboard the *S. S. Tjikarang*, 1931

Ruins of Old Panama City 1959, Helen Miller Bailey

CHAPTER FOUR

Settlement House Work Builds a Foundation:

From Revolution to Institution

The assassination of Pablo Seañez, a young, progressive officer, was ordered by General Pancho Villa as part of an internal power struggle and purge among his *Villanistas*. Fearing further violence, the Seañez family fled west from their homes in Chihuahua, near the end of the Mexican Revolution, which by 1917 had spilled over both sides of our shared border.

The survivors had made their way northwest to Los Angeles by the early 1920s. Here Mexican immigrants like Maria Seañez Cardoza, her husband Manuel Cardoza, and their surviving children, who had undergone a difficult and daunting pilgrimage to Southern California, faced a more welcoming atmosphere than in other American cities since workers were being hired in agriculture and manufacturing to serve the needs of the fast-growing population of over 1.2 million, an 1,100 percent increase over its 1900 census figures. The Cardozas and other twentieth century newcomers to California, of which 90 percent were of European descent, experienced the meteoric rise of Los Angeles and San Diego.

By the early 1930s, Mexican American residents of Los Angeles represented the largest minority, numbering nearly one hundred thousand. Until then, there had been plenty of work in the tire and auto manufacturing industries as well as in meat packing plants. However, all "bubbles" end and the Great Depression hit Californians particularly hard. As often happens, societal fears sought out scapegoats. Regardless of how "American" these Mexicans had become and how many were American born, millions were "repatriated" to Mexico, which California historian Kevin Starr described in his 2007 *California a History*, "a program that can only be described as ethnic cleansing . . . which foreshadowed the removal from the Pacific Coast in early 1942 of all people of Japanese ancestry, citizen and noncitizen alike."

Additionally, until the 1960s, people of color faced more challenges than most because many ethnic groups were barred by statute from living in several areas of Los Angeles County, and throughout the state. Knowledge of these property laws makes it easier to understand the concentration of Mexican American families on Los Angeles' Eastside. There they found one place poor families of any ethnicity could live and turn for help—All Nations Settlement House on East Sixth Street in downtown Los Angeles. According to the California Social Welfare Archives, All Nations was the largest and most effective social welfare organization operating in Los Angeles in those early years of the twentieth century. All Nations is where the relationship between the Seañez-Cardoza, Juárez, and Bailey families began.

The All Nations Settlement House was a project of the City Missionary Society of the Methodist Church and by 1918 had begun serving the needy immigrant population of Los Angeles. During the organization's most active period of the 1930s, Helen Miller and Henry Morle Bailey (he preferred Morle) were both volunteering at All Nations while teaching in Eastside schools during the day. We don't know if they met at All Nations, but Helen had just moved temporarily to LA in fall of 1930. She had been hired for one-year teaching assignments at a junior high school and Morle was teaching physics at Roosevelt High School.

Helen Lorraine Miller, the twenty-three-year-old historian/ sociologist from Modesto, California, and Henry Morle Bailey, the thirty-four-year-old physicist from Iowa, married on June 19, 1932 in Los Angeles. The ceremony was performed at a Methodist Episcopal church on 65th Street and witnessed by her mother Maude Piggott Miller and his sister Margaret Barnhilll.

In addition to volunteer teachers, social workers, and religious representatives, All Nations staffed a clinic with doctors, dentists, and nurses. Through the avid fundraising efforts of its first Pastor Bromley Oxnam, All Nations expanded from its original home in an abandoned church. He acquired land, equipped gymnasiums, playgrounds, libraries, and eventually operated two other centers in the Hollywood and the Hollenbeck Heights neighborhoods.

Helen became friends with the Seañez-Cardoza children who attended All Nations. She first befriended the eldest, Jose, who became her unofficial community aide, followed by the two younger brothers Jesus and Ricardo, and their sister Amparo. Because of Helen's ability to speak some Spanish, she was soon embraced by their parents Maria and Manuel and thus the Bailey and Seañez-Cardoza families became intertwined for many years.

Additionally, Helen and Morle mentored and foster-parented several young men from All Nations' markedly successful Boys Club, reported to have decreased delinquency by 65 percent between 1927 and 1930.

Abuelita Maria, had been sickened by years of war in her own country and devastated by the loss of her three younger brothers—Pablo, Nicolas, and Juan—who died in the *Revolucion* with tens of thousands of their countrymen. With the outbreak of WWII, she took her two youngest sons to Tijuana, for fear that these American born sons would be drafted into the Army, and she would lose them too.

Tragically, shortly after the family moved to Mexico, her son Jesus, a strong swimmer and athlete drowned in a heroic effort to help a woman caught in the undertow of treacherous surf off Rosarito Beach. His body was never recovered.

The second boy, teenager Ricardo, who had been born and raised in Los Angeles, insisted on returning home to join his older sister Amparo, who had by then married Alberto Juárez Sr., and was raising a young family of her own in East Los Angeles. At some point Amparo made arrangements for Ricardo to live with their teacher friends, the Baileys from All Nations. Ricardo thereby became a ward of Helen and Morle, who ensured he was able to complete his high school education. Morle and Ricardo made the long trek from the Bailey home in La Cañada to Roosevelt High School in Boyle Heights together each morning for two years. Those daily road trips created a bond between the two. Ricardo became very devoted to Morle.

While the Bailey's generosity is often hailed as extraordinary, it is important to understand conditions of the day which made taking homeless or at-risk children into one's home without legal authority a responsible course of action for these teachers.

Concern with child welfare and foster care declined in America's conservative 1920s' political climate. Likewise these topics were conspicuously missing from New Deal era reforms of the early 1930s. The absence of public focus on neglected and at-risk youth was then the norm when the US economy ground to a halt during the Great Depression. Hundreds of thousands of young men and boys were simply turned out of their homes because there wasn't enough food to feed the whole family. They could be found all around the country riding railroad cars, resting in hobo camps and doing odd jobs that might earn an apple or a nickel for a few hours' work.

Half a million Americans were homeless. Reading Steinbeck's *The Grapes of Wrath* or experiencing their desperation through photographer Dorothea Lange's *An American Exodus* provides some insight into the human experience during these troubled times and the poor treatment many of these unfortunate people endured. An example of prevailing public sentiment in California was the 1936 "Bums Blockade" set up by the Los Angeles Police Department. They closed off California borders for six weeks to migrants from the drought-devastated Mid-West states. "Bums" was a handle bestowed by a hardened nation on homeless Americans, most through no fault of their own.

Thus, very informal fostering practices were in place for many years before the contemporary child welfare bureaucracy was created in the years following WWII. The fact that the Baileys had teaching jobs during most of the 1930s and 1940s made them uniquely able to open their doors to many in need. It was not until 1962 that federal monies were offered to foster parents through the federal Aid to Families with Dependent Children program (AFDC).

Upon graduation from Roosevelt High School, just as *Abuelita* Maria feared, Ricardo was drafted and served in the South Pacific with the US Army's First Cavalry Division. During this time Helen continued her friendship with Amparo, who had been diagnosed with rheumatic fever. Through the intervention of the doctors at All Nations' clinic she was placed in a Salvation Army convalescent care facility. Helen interceded on Amparo's behalf with the American Red Cross so that her husband Alberto Sr., who was by that time also serving in the Army, could be released or stationed stateside due to his wife's condition and family hardship. Unfortunately the critical manpower needs at the height of the WWII demanded that Alberto Sr. and his infantry unit ship out along with nephew Ricardo's outfit. They became part of the American forces that fought in the liberation of the Philippines. Ricardo also served with the occupation forces in Japan.

After the war, Ricardo returned home and was again welcomed into the Bailey household in La Cañada and went to Glendale Community College on the GI Bill. Amparo and Helen worked out a unique arrangement for what would have then been considered "motherly" duties. On her morning commute to East Los Angeles College (classes then held at Garfield High School near the Cardoza-Juárez home in East Los Angeles), Helen would stop at Amparo's home and drop off Ricardo's laundry. A day later, Helen picked up his ironed shirts and laundry as she headed back up the mountain to the cabin in La Cañada.

Ricardo Cardoza, "Uncle Rick," as he was known to his biological nieces and nephews and later the Bailey grandchildren, met Minna Christoffersen in the Foreign Language Club at Glendale Community College. The two married and started their own family. Ricardo was in the Air Force Reserve and was recalled to serve as a noncommissioned officer stationed in San Antonio, Texas, at the outbreak of the Korean Conflict. Upon the family's return to California, Minna and Ricardo lived with the Baileys for a time. Working at a county detention center as a groundskeeper, Ricardo became interested in a career in public service. He returned to college at the University of Southern California and became a social worker for Los Angeles County—indeed, the first Latino to serve as a camp director and ultimately director of the East Los Angeles Regional Probation Department for the County of Los Angeles.

In October 2005, not long after Rick's death, both Minna Cardoza-Dyer and one of his two educator daughters, then Cal State Los Angeles Dean of Social Sciences Desdemona Cardoza, were interviewed for this tribute.

Minna recalled having talked more often to Morle than Helen during their temporary stay at the La Cañada cabin with their two young daughters. She described Morle as a really lovely man—very interested in her thoughts about America since she had immigrated from Denmark. She was impressed with how nicely he always spoke of Helen, who Minna described as "very harsh, blunt and always on guard." For a different perspective, Minna's nephew Alberto Juárez Jr. (and former Bailey student) described Helen as having "tremendous nervous energy," which she expressed by pointing her finger in the air saying, "Right, right, right," while scurrying across campus, usually with several students following at her heels.

Minna added, "When I think back, Helen must have been a stunning young woman, and I think had a come-on kind of a way with men." Helen was attractive with a Julia Roberts-sized smile and sparkling eyes to capture attention. She had a good figure and dressed with femininity. She had a favorite pink dress she was often photographed wearing. Even the Mexican peasant blouses and long skirts she took to wearing to school in her fifties, after the girlish figure was lost, combined with her little bit of a limp gave a seductive roll to her hips as she walked. Joel Busch, now retired history professor who Helen hired in 1972, described Helen as "sort of floating into my classroom when she sat in to evaluate my teaching progress."

Minna described those years as fraught with discrimination. She recalled Helen faced prejudice as a female PhD educator, who couldn't find work for a time though Morle, without a doctorate, was steadily employed. Minna is convinced Helen only overcame the bias of the day because of her tenacity.

When Minna came to Los Angeles from Copenhagen, she sailed through her community college classes with ease, "I knew Latin and French and soon earned my PhD in Germanic languages and linguistics and later taught in graduate school at Immaculate Heart College." Minna remembers Rick visiting Helen less and less over the years, "After our girls Desdemona and Anita were born, Rick got more and more involved with his own family in Mexico."

Desdemona Cardoza, a striking woman even when a teary gentleness replaced her professional demeanor, spoke of her father Ricardo Cardoza and his relationship with the Baileys. She recalled one of the many times Helen and Morle babysat her and her sister Anita. "Morle was sitting in a chair reading while my sister and I sat playing nearby in the living room. Helen came bounding into the room and jumped into Morle's lap and began kissing his face all over. He seemed embarrassed, and motioned towards Anita and me. Helen turned to us and pleaded, 'Oh girls, you don't mind do you?'"

Like her mother and sister, Desdemona Cardoza was a college professor for much of her career; additionally, she has served many years in administration at Cal State University Los Angeles. While her first love was teaching, she explained, "I realized early on how many more students I could actually help in my role as dean." Dr. Cardoza was appointed Provost of the campus, which supports about twenty thousand students. In 2010 she transitioned to a more strategic role for the California State University system as a consultant to the chancellor's office.

Her sister Anita Cardoza Flemington has been an educator since 1974. With a doctoral degree in education from Pepperdine University, she has specialized in bilingual education and second language acquisition. Dr. Flemington is professor of education in the College of Education and Organizational Leadership at the University of La Verne.

It seems reasonable to infer that this deeply held value of service evidenced by the careers of both daughters of Ricardo Cardoza was inspired, to some degree, by the generosity and friendship extended to their family by the Baileys.

Desdemona recalled vacationing for a couple of weeks at the Bailey's property on Balboa Island every summer for nearly a decade. Since two homes stood on the lot, there was plenty of room for one or two of the Bailey boys to be in residence at the same time with their own families. In response to a reporter's questioning what qualified a young man to be considered a Bailey boy, Helen responded, "They must have lived with us for two or more years." Rick Cardoza and Ted Bailey had been teenage buddies since they lived together as brothers for over fifteen years. While they both attended Glendale College, they often coasted downhill (at least part way) from the Bailey cabin to campus to save on gas in their old jalopy of a car.

Other memories of Dr. Bailey's relationship with his mother Amparo, his Uncle Rick Cardoza, and their families were offered by Pasadena City College Political Science adjunct Professor Alberto Juárez Jr. He recalled fondly the day his Uncle Rick graduated and

Helen came to pick up his mom to take her to the commencement exercises at Glendale College. On a whim, Helen said to Amparo, "Let's bring Butch [Alberto's nickname] along." Amparo resisted the idea because the boy was in his play clothes and there was no time to clean him up and put on his Sunday outfit. Helen insisted, "Oh, Amparo, he's just a little boy, no one will ever notice." Juárez recalled, "She was right, nobody did notice me, but I did take notice of my first college graduation ceremony and it left a lasting impression on me."

In 1959, Juárez received a $50 scholarship from the Armando Castro Scholarship Fund and enrolled in Helen's Latin American History class at East Los Angeles College. At the behest of Helen, he went on to graduate from the University of California Los Angeles. Juárez served as an aide to Los Angeles Mayor Tom Bradley, and later transitioned into education, as did so many influenced by Doc Bailey's calling.

In a 2012 interview the Pasadena City College political science professor made a bold statement which others have hinted at, although with less specificity. He recalled a large glass display case that stood against the west wall of the student entrance to the Social Science Department at East Los Angeles College. On view during her tenure were many Mexican artifacts collected during Helen's numerous trips to Mexico and other Latin American countries. Juárez somewhat seriously proposed the contents of this glass display case, curated by this female, Anglo social science department chair at East Los Angeles College, was indeed the first Chicano Studies Department, "She helped us to become Chicanos and more fully respect and embrace our *Mexicanidad*. One could make the case that Helen Miller Bailey was the cornerstone of the Chicano student movement in California."

As one of the founders of the Mexican American Student Association (MASA) on the ELAC campus, Juárez enjoyed the validation of having Helen serve as the faculty sponsor of the group, arguably the first Chicano club on a college campus,

> *She truly was an Anglo woman with the soul of a Mexican. Through MASA we brought together a core group of students such as Antonia Hernandez, Mexican American Legal Defense Fund (MALDEF) president/ general counsel and California Foundation CEO; Dr. Gil Cardenas of Notre Dame; Dr. Raul Cardoza, now emeritus community college president; Dr. David Almada, former mayor of Monterey Park and distinguished educator; Richard Avila, former California deputy attorney general and ELAC history professor; and a score of other soon-to-be civic leaders and activists. Unfortunately, I think we may have taken her for granted at the time—Doc Bailey— the treasure among us. She was so unassuming—so down to earth with everyone.*

Years later, MASA, United Mexican American Students (UMAS), Mexican American Student Confederation (MASC), and other California college campus groups with a shared focus on improving educational quality and opportunity for Latinos(as) merged at the pivotal April 1969 conference at University of California Santa Barbara. The resulting organization, *El Movimiento Estudiantil Chicano de Aztlan* (MECHA), became an institutionalized student group on many high school, college, and university campuses— both in the Southwest and the Ivy League (e.g., Harvard, Yale, and Princeton). By all accounts, the work done at the Santa Barbara conference laid the groundwork for Chicano Studies programs throughout the country.

At East Los Angeles College in 1996, Armida Torres Avila carried on her old professor's tradition by sponsoring the Mathematics, Engineering, Science Achievement Program (MESA) until her retirement in 2013. Aimed at helping single-parent heads of households preparing to enter the workforce, the program provided a support system both on and off campus.

The great educational institutions of Los Angeles and, more generally, California, have benefitted from educators mentored by Dr. Helen Miller Bailey. The Bailey's alma mater, the University of Southern California, can boast of an impressive alumni cohort of Bailey devotees.

Other programs at private colleges around the country, such as the Chicano Studies founded by Dr. Gilbert Cardenas at Notre Dame, have been enhanced by Bailey protégés.

Helen Lorraine Miller and Henry Morle Bailey
Wedding Portrait June 1932

European Fortress Sketch, Helen Miller Bailey

CHAPTER FIVE

A-Wheel in Europe: 1936 Journal Excerpts

To be sure, the day after school let out for the summer, the Baileys were headed for a new adventure, not to return until just before classes resumed in the fall. Not only was each precious hour used to satisfy Helen's desire to experience other cultures, but every dime as well, "Having saved upwards of a thousand dollars, we are full of plans to go cruising on the Mediterranean to Constantinople. But such a trip would leave us no money to live on in September." So it was youth hostels, cycling, travelling in a donkey cart, crowding in third-class steamship births across the Atlantic, driving the Pan American highway from California to Guatemala and Mexico, struggling with bed bugs, fleas, and surviving Helen's fierce seasickness, and Morle's crutches.

These challenges might scare off the more timid among us, but not Helen and Morle (her precious Petie). It should be noted here that for years Morle used a cane or crutches until 1955 when the polio virus cruelly confined him to a wheelchair and retirement. This handsome, USC graduated science teacher was not immune to the indiscriminate siege against the legs that could no longer support his tall, athletic frame.

Helen's eighty-page travel journal from this summer describes how she cycled through Germany in 1936 with various groups, some organized by the founders of the American youth hostels program. This was the very year of the Berlin Olympic Games, "which the Nazis made into an immensely impressive spectacle—raw propaganda with Goebbels at the controls and Hitler playing *normal*," explained ELAC History Professor Joel Busch, "At the time, Germany was experiencing what some called an economic miracle after emerging from a decade of ruinous hyperinflation caused by unrealistic WWI reparations demanded by the allied countries, combined with a disastrous internal monetary policy."

The story Helen tells of this summer's trip provides insight into her courage, stamina, and the strength of her marriage.

This is the adventure of Helen Miller Bailey and Henry Morle Bailey abroad on the continent of Europe in the summer of 1936. I am in touch with the American Youth Hostel Association, which has had articles published in the Readers Digest, Scholastic, and Time, about the hiking and cycling Youth Movement in Europe, the inns or hostels provided for members in France, Germany, and Scandinavia, and the new group in America. These people under the leadership of Isabel and Monroe Smith

*of Northfield, Massachusetts, have founded a chain of
such inns in New England for American youth afoot or on
cycles. Last year, also, a group of American "hostelers"
went to Europe and had a fine time cycling down the
Rhine, etc. Last year we were in touch with Monroe Smith
to get information about Youth Hostels in Ireland. We
subsequently joined the Irish Youth Hostel Association,
and used our membership to advantage while travelling
by donkey cart in Ireland.*

A Summer Apart to Bring Europe to Her Classroom

*The Youth Hostel Cycling group in Europe, therefore,
comes to be the solution for my problem. Morle meanwhile
has been reading articles in the Geographic magazine
about fishing fleets off the coast of Normandy and Brittany,
about pirate coves on the Channel Islands of Guernsey,
Jersey, Alderney and Sark, about St. Malo, home of the
Corsaires [pirates]. He wants to watch small boats come
into picturesque harbors, to sit and smoke his pipe while
fishing fleets dock at old quays. So do I— for a day, but
not for all summer.*

*I want to get close to the people, walk along the roads,
stay in small villages, where Americans never go. Cycling
is the solution for what I want to do in Europe—but is out of
the question for Morle. So after long discussion we decide
to spend half the summer apart—for the first time. I will
cycle with the Youth Hostel group in Germany till August 1,
then come back to France and meet Morle for some touring
together in August. When we land we will go from Havre*

down the Norman Coast to St. Malo, where Morle will find a place to stay and a permanent summer address. Then I will leave him for Germany. Here at the headquarters of the International Youth Hostel Association, I will meet the Smiths and the rest of the American cycling group. All plans were very indefinite after that.

Already I have sent the American Youth Hostel Association $162. Two is for this year's adult membership, thirty is for a scholarship and leadership fund, to which I gladly make contribution. Thirty more is for a $25 bicycle, to be ready for me in Cologne, and for a new rucksack and sheet bag to carry my things on the bike. The remaining hundred dollars is paid into the group expense fund, and is supposed to cover my complete expenses as long as I am with the group of cyclists . . . I expect to get at least fifty dollars of it back to live on in August.

Two round-trip bus fares—Montreal and Los Angeles @ $82	*$164.40*
Food and overnights on bus both ways for two people	*48.00*
Two round-trip steamship fares, Montreal, Canada to Havre, France	*309.00*
Federal tax on tickets	*10.00*
Tips on boat—both ways	*8.00*
American Express traveler's checks	
Morle	*$130.00*
Helen	*$100.00*
Total	*$925.40*

This runs ... much higher than any trip we ever took—and does not include $50 spent for film—but we must bring back $50 of the $230, or, we don't live till October's pay day. Maybe I can sell the bicycle for something.

We are pleased and surprised at Montreal. It is such a combination of France, England, and America. Following our custom—the way we have seen Mexico City, New York, London, Glasgow, etc.—we take all the street car lines in town and go to both ends (of the city).

As I am sitting on board the S.S. Montrose, writing this epic, I am exceedingly depressed in spirit about such boats—we got on at 10 a.m. and immediately said, "Oh, oh, third class looks pretty bad"—the smallest cabin, the least deck space, the dirtiest unpainted ship passages. But there are only 200 in steerage third—so we do not feel crowded or unhappy as we start down the lovely St. Lawrence toward Quebec. Though the third class dining room is in the bottom of the ship, down long airless, smelling runways through the crew's quarters, the good food turns out to be unusually so—thanks to French chefs—the same food, in fact, that is sold to the tourist class.

A Migratory Canadian Workforce Circa 1936

We are at the table with a peppy little matron from Ottowa, "goin' 'ome" to see her folks, after "all these long years out 'are"—and a Jugo-Slavian steel mill worker, who has had his feet and legs badly frozen in Canada, and is going home to Azgreb to live off his wife's people. He remains bundled up like an Eskimo, but speaks enough English to tell me about how the Croats are ruining Yugo-Slavia by intrigue against the Serbs on the side of Mussolini, and adds to my information about the Karageargivitch Kings—Everyone else in Third Class is "goin' 'ome"—some just for a visit with the old folks and some, disgusted with the cold in Canada, are going back to dear old "Hengland" for good. We are the only Americans in Third Class. There is a large group of non-English speaking Finns and Swedes, lumberjacks, who have made a tidy sum in the north woods and are ready to go back to the old farms. They have a great many shy, fair-haired children. One English family from Saskatchewan is going back to London to "put their sons out to trade." (Poor kids—it seems as if half the crew on the English-run boat are kids 14 to 18, who have been "put out to the trade of able seamen" under the cruel English apprentice system.)

I talk and talk about the American public school system—compulsory till 18—but all these besodden cockneys, from the London streets, originally, can see nothing better for their sons, even in Canada. In the course of all this, we seem to pick up, as special friends, a young Swiss engineer, working for General Motors in America, but going for a holiday, and two Russian communists. The Swiss, Mr. Seewer, has cycled all through the Alpine hostels and has much advice and information about the cycling. The Russians have the usual single track minds of communists—they get right back to the Soviet no matter where the conversation starts. One of them has a lovely child, a boy about 18, who is a genius at the piano—the boy was raised in Canada, but his father is taking him to Moscow to put him in the Russian Conservatory of Music.

One of the tourist class stewards was in the anti-narcotic squad of the English army in Egypt, and worked for Russell Pasha, of League of Nations fame (he of my PhD thesis).

Mme. Bougant Promises to Take Good Care of Morle in Medieval St. Malo

At last it is Friday. We were given our landing cards today, and are to get into Havre Sunday morning early. No one knows where to tell us to go then, and we have cashed no money into French francs. It will take me most of two days to get to Cologne from St. Malo—Tonight there is actually to be a show and concert, after seven depressing days, but since it is up in the snooty tourist section, I have refused to play the harmonica— (not even "Home on the Range.")

July 7—We will be together only two more days. The garcon helps us get money changed and catch the trolley to Mont. St. Michel. We see the famous mountain island shrine above the tide lands as we go out . . . it is all as charming and picturesque as it was ever purported to be. We buy a book telling the whole history of this place, from its founding in AD 709.

July 8—At St. Malo, home of the Corsairs—(who) certainly had it fine here—with the rocky harbor the fortified islands, and the closely walled town which would have kept all other roving pirates away from St. Malo. We find the real town . . . inside the medieval wall. Through the battlement is the gate of St. Vincent by which we enter the narrow cobbled streets.

Morle is delighted with the harbor, the boats, and the town itself. Here he will stay for the three weeks while I am with the Youth Hostelers. Mme. Bougant treats us to beer and promises to take good care of Morle while I am gone. She and her little maid laughingly promise to keep him away from all pretty girls. Tonight I pack the knapsack with all my stuff, and get ready to go tomorrow. I find Morle getting upset at my going off alone, and feeling quite lonesome already.

July 10—Well, well, well! What is there to write or not write about third class railway compartments on the international night train north from Paris. Six people— two Americans, two Germans, two French —intensely amorous gentlemen—two borders to cross, with military passport, baggage, and foreign money inspection at each border (Belgium/Germany) — 'nuff said.

I barely catch the train—having to run with my knapsack bouncing behind me. The train is tiny and pre-war—and stops at some little industrial town every five minutes while people get on and off. Here is my little town at the bottom of a canyon. I have my first chance to spring my well-practiced sentence, "KÖnnen Sie mir sagen wo die Jugend Herbaergeist?"—Everyone points to a castle on top the hill—and I start slowly climbing up—first a steep cobbled street, then steps and finally a woodland path. Three boys come along behind me at the castle gate—I ask my sentence again—they crowd around excitedly and tell me in school-book English that another American lady is here waiting for me.

The First International Youth Hostel

I enter the castle gates with them—needless to describe this lovely old palace, the home of the first international youth hostel. Hilariously they bring me the other American lady——who turns out to be a badly sunburned hosteler—a game sport who has been three months hostelling on a cycle in Europe and now is here waiting for Isabel and Monroe Smith so she can join the group canoeing down the Danube. She is delighted to see me, shows me the old bedroom in the castle with its cove bed where she has been sleeping as the only foreign lady guest.

I am privileged to stay here, says Mrs. Schirrmann, the wife of the founder of all the Youth Hostels, who comes down to greet me surrounded by four flaxen-haired infants. All the boys, it seems, are here in a compulsory camp—part of Hitler's effort to combine boys of all classes and all geographic districts in summer camps. They have a special end of the castle provided just for such camps.

Two little boys from Sweden come in on cycles while we are all eating at long tables in the courtyard—They are cycling through Germany, though they seem about 12 or 13. They speak school-book English, but seem to have no trouble with German. I meet two Americans, leaders of the CCC Camp (California Conservation Corps). Captain Bennet is full of ideas for hostels in California. A young teacher, here with the boys (Mr. Swachenberg) tells me all about this, and of his own plans to bring a group of these same boys to California.

Then suddenly the word goes around that the Americans are at the station in Altena. Soon they're standing in the courtyard singing "Old McDonald had a Farm." These here tonight are all going to France. They are all from colleges in the East, and a little too "collegiate" for me. There are twenty-six of them and they crowd the hostel. I sleep with two others in a great walled-in carved bed in a room from the 16th century—a tiled stove place, many brass pots, and windows overlooking the town of Altena. One of them is Helen Conley, secretary of the whole group—a Mount Holyoke girl. She is under the impression that I am going to start a whole chain of hostels in Southern California.

July 15—All the Americans are lined up, ready to go to church in the town. So I go along—a very plain little Lutheran church with hard, narrow pews. On the side wall was a big gold plaque which said, "From this Church there died, for King and Fatherland, in the war of 1814–'15 these heroes"—and then six names. On the other side another "From this church, etc., just the same—in the War of 1866, these heroes" —and then seven names. On the side at the back a little different plaque for 1870–'71 with about 15 names, and then in front by the alter—a great one for 1914–'18—more names than I could count from where I sat.

After supper, Monroe Smith and fifty more American hostelers are gathered in the main room for a meeting. He is a charming personality; everything swings into shape— with no hurry, fuss or bother. Groups are organized, finances arranged, and everyone sent to bed. Monroe asked me to be up at 7:00 to talk to him personally. Next morning, he tells me of his hopes for hostels in California and suggests people I should contact in September.

While the 50 or so bicycles are being given out, I am able to keep the date I had set with some school girls of the Hochschule in Altena and go with them to English class. The director of the school knows I'm coming from my letters, but they have not warned the teacher, who is cross. But she is sweet as peaches when she finds out that I am a high school teacher (with a PhD). She has me talk to the class in English about schools at home—very slowly and clearly I answer questions. She herself does not approve of free compulsory education in liberal culture up to the age of 18 for the masses. But she thanks me most heartily when I must leave, and allows several girls to take all my stuff down to the station, where the bicycles are assembled. I am given one with a new knapsack, an unbleached muslin sack for sleeping, and a small handle bar thing called a wanderbag. We have a nice hot meal at a café first. Then we are off.

The group itself surprises and pleases me. Sprague and Peggy Curtis are young instructors at Smith College, and the seven girls are either graduates from or students at Smith. They are not at all snobby, and take me in good heartedly in spite of my advanced years, Western accent and inexperience at the bicycle. (How well I get along with these girls, with their private girls' school, private girls' college, money, and society backgrounds—I am pleased and surprised at myself, usually so intolerant of all these girls stand for but real people are so much the same the world over.)

The cycle itself is beautiful, but that makes it no easier for me to get up the long climb out of the canyon of Altena and over the ridge. I am so discouraged—the others get so far ahead—I run out of breath—my legs ache—oh, it is impossible. Why did I ever have this hair brained idea? But then we hit a town called Liedenschild and suddenly we go down, down, down, through beautiful green hills dotted with white farm houses and finally into a village named Kiesper. At 8:00 p.m. we find the Herberge in the town of Wipperfishr. It is a new building like an elementary school in LA. It is crowded with a group of little girls on an excursion. But we are given a small room with nine hard bunks.

Up at 6:00 in the morning I find the sun shining gaily—so I go off to paint near the house where we ate last night and find the group breakfasting. Three others and myself want to cycle. They say it is 18 kilometers to Remagen where we must catch the 11:22 boat to Mainz, so we set merrily off. The villages are quaint, charming, and very old-world. The Zeppelin Hindenburg passes above me—I stop often to take movies, quaint winding streets, churches in the middle of the street, children playing, people working in gardens. I enjoy myself more thoroughly than any day yet. Then suddenly I'm informed we must cross the railroad bridge and get to a town on the other side in seven minutes to catch the boat. Such a mad scramble up a steep hill and then to get the heavily loaded cycle across the high bridge and down the other side!

The others are just ahead of me, but never have I hurried so breathlessly—coasting down a steep hill, with no brakes on—honking everyone out of my way. I cycle madly right on to the gangplank and step on to the boat just as it leaves the wharf. Passengers crowd around me,

Good News from Ghent to Aix" (Robert Browning poem).

July 19—The sun is actually shinning, the country is all set out to grain, with colors and shadows in golds and purples. I stop often to get pictures of people harvesting, travelling sometimes with other girls, but mostly alone. We go through very heavy woods, and into Darmstadt, to find the Jugend Herberge in an old school house. As the girls come in, one by one, all are hot and tired. Seven of us decide to go swimming. While splashing around, I picked up two young men who had seen me giving out in the middle of the lake. When we all gave up and went into dress, my two prince charmings came out in the uniforms of state police(!), and were soon joined by another—So I go merrily down the street, through a thunder storm, escorted by three soldiers. They Shanghai me and take me out to dinner. The seven lost maidens, sitting in a café drinking Rhine wine, see me thus go by, and the stock I have invested in Smith College goes up several points.

July 20—We bike into Heidelberg by 4. Seven hours on the road for 60 kilometers is very good for me. Here in the courtyard of the Herberge, around the great old castle, other Hitler Jugend (Hitler Youth) crowd around as we come in. The fact that I speak German so very comically, that I teach in Los Angeles, California, where the movie stars live, and that I have students who can write to them in English endears me to the hearts of the Hitler Jugend, and some of them accompany me to sketch in the afternoon, and down town after our dinner of soup—I am continually talking about Los Angles, about American schools, about making water colors—in slow, painful English.

July 23—I am sitting on top of a hill on the edge of the Black Forest, overlooking the town and valley of Gernsbach—The big church on the hill, opposite, is tolling for a burial, and the sound of bells comes across to where I am. Although it rained yesterday, Eleanor Crane and I, the slow ones, started out before 10:00, in a terrible downpour, and got soaking wet. A few miles along my wet tire caught on a wet railroad track, and spilled me very badly, by far the worst fall I've had. It was several minutes before I could go on, I was so badly shaken up. We went on through lighter and lighter rain till it finally cleared and we went up this river valley in the sunshine. Here we met three girls from Belgium, touring Germany by cycle. We meet up with the rest of our group, who had not passed us on the road, and yet they were all here ahead of us, rowing over our slowness. They later explained they had all come on the train because of the rain. The Jugend Herberge is in the old town jail. Four of us sleep in each cell—myself in with the Belgians. The walk between the cells is filled with tables, and it is a very jolly prison, with such a nice family in charge.

Next morning I put on the dress I bought in Heidelberg, and all the Germans posed with me for pictures and movies. I also took a great many movies of people in the streets, and got a nice sketch from a friendly door yard. Here the people gave me a whole bag of plums and allowed me to ride back to the Herberge on the back of one of their work horses, while it pulled a cart of firewood.

Helen Miller Bailey, Germany 1936

July 24—We were supposed to just climb a little hill, coast all the way down into Baden Baden, 35 kilometers, an easy day's ride. I do not reach the top of the hill (as big and seemingly as long as Cajon Pass[a several mile mountain pass northeast of Los Angeles on Highway 5]) until after Noon, walking and pushing the bike all the way up. Exhausted, I coast down into Baden Baden, to be met by a sign "Offenburg, 42 kilometers"—Sadly, I paddle along alone for hours and hours, though through lovely country. The road is crowded with ox carts loaded with grain, making cycling very difficult.

Then as I cautiously tried to go round one, a car came whizzing by and side swiped me, knocking me off the bicycle onto my already sore knee bending my handle bars, knocking my tire out of the rim, and scaring me into pink fits. The car went rudely on, but the farmers in the ox cart picked me and the cycle up and carried me about 2 kilometers to the next village. Here they told the story while many kind people crowded round, a repair man fixed by cycle in less than an hour and everyone got me well started on the road again. When I finally arrived at the town of Offenburg, a man hailed me from an inn. He turned out to be the kind (!) man who had run me down.

Helen and bicycle repairman, Germany 1936

I awake, after a restless night, as tired as I was when I went to bed. We have 64 kilometers to go today—the longest trip yet—and it is raining. But I start out, and make the trip slowly and painfully, down a valley in the hills and into the pleasant town of Freiburg by 5:00. Here I found my commissary partner and we joyfully bought meals of frankfurters and potato salad from the Herberge kitchen for the group.

Other causes for joy were the letters, the first mail I've yet had since Altena—two letters from Morle, two from students of mine (Elaine Ericksson and Richard Irwin) and a note from Mr. Seewer, asking me again to Winterthur, near Zurich. I answered them all, accepting the Swiss invitation for July 28, and went wearily to bed. There has been a big church festival in Freiburg today, and the hostel is crowded with young people from towns nearby. The only room left for us is on army cots, spread out in the halls, on the stair landings, and in the washroom.

We were to go 50 kilometers today through hilly country, and my body simply refuses. The younger members of the group (those four who are from 18 to 20) have decided to stay over and paint Freiburg red for Sunday and come to Kadern Schneiden on the train in the late afternoon. One of these debutantes, Ellen, has slept in an expensive hotel for a rest, and is keeping the room today, so we can all have a hot bath. As ordered by Sprague Curtis, a medical student, I have a glorious rest in the luxury of a real featherbed and get to wash my hair in hot water. I was sorry to lose this day's cycling in the warm sunshine, as I will only have one more day before we are in Switzerland.

We get off the train in Kandern at 7:30 p.m. only to find to our, and especially my, anguish that we are 17 kilometers from Haltingen into the hills. It was growing dark, the others were expecting us—nothing to do but start out and go. All the village people along the way were promenading in their Sunday clothes. We arrived with me trailing behind—only to find a second tragedy the Jugend Herberge is on top a mountain six kilometers up. I simply cannot go further—I am going to stay in an inn in the town. The four young girls think this will be an adventure and we find a little place on the old square, where we can phone the others at the Jugend Herberge.

As we go farther and farther south, the country is more rural, the people more of the peasant type—with less show of militarism—even the kids are not all marching Hitler Jugends. The hostels are dirtier, less convenient, etc., but everything is more easy-going.

We are to go straight south to the Rhine and then east along the Swiss border to Waldshut—a crossing place to Switzerland—much better—I keep up with the other girls all day. It pours rain in the afternoon, and it is fun. The last day I am cycling with the girls, we stop under a farmer's great shed and wait for an hour for the rain to quit. The Jugend Herberge in Waldshut, my last in Germany, is called "Cloud's Rest." It is surely in the clouds—so misty, wet, and dripping we cannot see the view, nor even the waterfalls—only the Swiss chalet-type drafty Herberge. The old wood stove works badly, the wood is wet, water must be brought in kettles from the brook. But I am able to serve up baked potatoes with a cream sauce of milk, onions, chives, and Swiss cheese.

In the morning we are all off downhill to the town and the international bridge, where everyone on both sides is very kind and interested, and we are allowed to take our cycles into Switzerland free of any toll or tax. Here at the bridge, a sign in one direction, "Zurich" and in another, "Wipperfürth." So I must leave the group for good here, as they are going to a place called Zug and then back to Germany in two days. I do not relish the idea of travelling alone. It is 45 kilometers to Wipperfürth and it is alternately rain and shine, and though I get dripping wet, it is a very pleasant journey—such pretty country. Mr. Seewer's mother has written me the phone number to call when I get to Wipperfürth—which I do from a pastry

shop. She will not have me staying in a hotel. With Mr.
Seewer in 1935 in America, she was invited to stay in
an American home, and wants to pass on the favor. Mr.
Seewer and his father come home and I must tell all about
my trip, read them Morle's letters, and show my pictures.
These kind people have planned for every moment so that
I shall see everything. It is surely nice to be so well taken
care of.

July 30—I miss the morning train to Lucerne (my next
stop on the Seewer-planned itinerary) so cannot go until
3:30, but I certainly see Zurich at a breakneck pace of
strides a meter long. I catch the train punctually and am
off to Lucerne—unable to thank these very kind people
enough. How nice that a chance acquaintance made on
a boat, largely by Morle, should lead to such kindness
towards me on the part of the whole family.

Basking in the "International Spirit"

Arriving in Lucerne in two hours, I merely look for
the sign of the cyclists association on little hotels near
the station, and find a nice one with a café attached.
Lucerne is so beautiful, just at sunset, it is useless to try
to describe it—only I feel so exceedingly lonely, having left
the charming family in Wipperfürth and Zurich, having
left the Curtis Group girls at Waldshut, and not having
seen Morle for nearly a month.

August 1—I am surely glad I stayed in Switzerland as
today is the big Swiss National holiday and Independence
Day. First there is the big Saturday market in Lucerne,

along both sides of the river where it flows into the lake. Then there are the banners and flags flying everywhere, the girls in national costumes everywhere on the streets, selling little flags for the Anti-Tubercular Society—the bands playing, everyone out in their best—I walk (much longer, faster, and with bigger steps than if I hadn't been getting so much practice lately) all round the lake shore, through the market. I fall for a curio or two, buy some postcards, take a lot of movies, and still have time to paint the famous covered bridge in the center of town.

August 2—Swiss prices are so high because Switzerland is on the gold standard and we are off. But I dine near the station for two francs as soon as I get off the bicycle and begin, going around on foot without a knapsack, everyone gazes at me as a public curiosity. I certainly do look tough, in my divided culottes dress, my old sweaters, and the brown and orange cap, now sad and soggy looking. My shoes are all out at the sole, my socks faded, and my legs badly bruised and scratched. Also, in spite of the continuous rain, I have managed to get pretty sunburned. I sit quietly in a corner café and watch the holiday merriment—the flags waving, band playing and fireworks going off until I climb wearily up many flights of stairs to bed.

Sunday morning I planned to have the cycle sent directly, to take the bus to the League of Nations building and merely stroll around town the rest of the day. But with this unexpected sunshine in my soul, I pack my two sacks, pay the bill, and hurry back to the station to get my bicycle out of the baggage department before they send it away. I am on the bike and away, out of the city towards the League Building. There is a sign over the gate that visitors are not admitted until 2:30 so I go on cycling up a slow hill till I find myself in a clover field, looking out over a panorama of farms and valleys to snow-covered Alps beyond. Here I unpack and sit in the middle of the clover, making a sketch—and then simply lying in the sunshine, letting the warmth and peace soak all through me.

I head back to the League building where a French speaking guide, who took me, a party of one, through the offices, and to see all the very fine murals of various types of labor throughout the world, each one donated by a different country. Geneva seems to be very modern; it has been "put on the map" by the League of Nations. I certainly enjoyed my Sunday there, basking in the "international spirit." I returned to the station and sent the bicycle by express to Paris, where we both arrive at 6:00 a.m. My train to St. Malo leaves at 9:30 p.m. so I can bicycle and see Paris for 15 hours.

Gathering Posters for the Classroom

A kind lady asks all about the cycle. My French, which I had found so rusty in Geneva, comes rushing back, and I tell her what I want to see in Paris. The Louvre is closed on Mondays—perhaps I will come again another year and see the inside. With a map of the "Metro"—the subways of Paris—I start out to go 20 kilometers until 4:00 p.m.— cycling when the traffic is heavy, pushing the bike on foot up the Champs Elysees and the Rue de Rivoli—paying little brats a few centimes to watch the knapsacks while I go into Notre Dame Cathedral and climb the Eiffel Tower. I cycled up the Mont Martre, student section, or Latin Quarter, walked along the Tuileries gardens and waited an hour for the Guignol puppet show. At four, I cycle exhaustedly back to Mont Parnasse station and pay to get my bike up an elevator and into the express office where I buy my ticket to St. Malo.

Rid of the bike and the knapsacks I go wandering about the rather old section of Paris, near the station— walking steadily for more than an hour and finding a nice place for a good French dinner. By the time I have walked back to the station, worked the information bureau for seven posters of Brittany, it is after 8, so I drowse an hour in the dirty third class waiting room, write a letter to Seewers, and here is the train.

The third class car I get is almost empty so I have a compartment all to myself and stretch out luxuriously— alas, history repeats itself—once in Mexico we were peacefully sleeping on a third class car when the officials decided to unhook that car and go on without it. Here at the city of Chartres, I was almost stranded for the same reason, and when I drearily changed to the forward cars, they were so crowded there was no room even to sit down. The two hours I slept before noon were the only ones I slept that night.

The next two days in St. Malo were devoted mainly to resting. I stayed in bed in Morle's musty little room at the Café du Printemps almost all day—only coming up for air for dinner.

August 5—I am up and walking around the battlements, going to see the boats and docks. Morle has been revving up to show me the diary he has so faithfully kept. We are busy trying to decide whether I shall go on another cycling trip alone into Brittany while Morle goes to Jersey. All the people at the little inn try to persuade me not to go away again—the Madame, the three little maids, the boarder who speaks English (a factory worker here in St. Malo), and her much younger husband (a stevedore) as well as the laundry lady next door, and the baker across the lane—all almost hysterical asking me not to leave "Monsieur" alone again. I want very badly to make the trip as soon as I am rested—do some cycling in rural France. I have not yet decided.

Angine Epidemique

August 10—All plans and decisions were postponed, beginning last Thursday when Morle came down with an "epidemic," as Madame Bougant called it—first a sore throat, then fever and upset stomach, and finally his throat closed up all together, making even breathing difficult. Since it seems something caught through contagion (he was so rested and in such fine condition when I came back two days before) and all our French friends call it the "angine epidemique," so I am afraid immediately of diphtheria. But angine epidemique in our dictionary means Quincy sore throat. All we can do is keep him wrapped up and breathing and wait for the abscess to break. This is a process which would almost be funny if it

*were not as pathetically hard on Morle to have to suffer
so in this dirty, smelly, unsanitary little dump with fleas
in the bed.*

*But everyone is so helpful, the big wood stove in the
little kitchen is kept going all the time to heat water for hot
compresses (the same water, in the same basin, floating
the same rag, heated over and over). The baker, the cider
carter, even the old lady who sells fish, are interested and
full of helpful suggestions. The windows must be kept
tight closed, the bed piled high with covers (under which
other people with angine have slept?). The "Monsieur"
must be forced to sweat constantly and filled up on hot
grog (rum, sugar, and hot water), an old stocking must be
kept round his neck, an onion poultice on his chest. The
stevedore friend, rushing in from unloading codfish off a
sailboat from the Newfoundland banks, brings eucalyptus
candy as his special treat—I do the very best I can to keep
everybody friendly and even close the windows quickly
when anyone knocks on the room door. I am a poor nurse
at best, not having the patience nor the knack and to
work under such bad sanitary conditions, in such crowded
quarters, while struggling to make myself understood in
a foreign language.*

*Anyway, Morle came out alive, as the abscess broke
Sunday night, and he has been up today, able to talk and
walk and even swallow small pieces of hard French bread.
The surprise of his sudden recovery, combined with a
mess of raw clams which had been too long out of the
water reacted on my poor old stomach, and has laid me
up with a bad case of land-seasickness. The decision to go*

to Brittany and to Jersey is still postponed, though I have gained some information about festivals in Brittany called "Pardons," a series of which are given to St. Christine in several small towns on August 15—next Saturday.

While Morle was sick I was able to paint four pictures on the larger sketch pad I bought in Montreal, one of the battlements at the "Grande Porte" to the town, while I sat in a little café where Morle had made friends with the waiters—one after a long walk clear out to the end of the breakwater and in to the lighthouse, where I painted some bright-sailed boats in reds and oranges against the gray of the walled town—one of a little street near ours, just at dusk—and then on Sunday afternoon, with the sun shining clear, I climbed to the top of the St. Malo Cathedral to sketch and photograph the panorama. I also went on Saturday with the maid, Andrae, and Madame Bougant to the St. Malo market, where I helped them buy green produce, butter, eggs, and especially shell fish (a whole square is reserved especially for the St. Malo fish market) and where I got what ought to be good movies of them doing the buying.

August 11—Well, here I am alone out on a trip with the bicycle into Brittany. Morle was so much better this morning, and full of his own plans to go to the Island of Jersey, and I have been such a patient nurse, it seems all right for me to go off, to seek the free open air again. We packed the two suit cases, and a knapsack each. We will leave the cases with Mme. Bougant until we both return next Sunday en route to Cherbourg on the 18th.

The closest "Pardon" festival is in a small coast town called Perros-Guirec—170 kilometers if I go on an interesting way. I can cycle Tuesday, through Friday—see the festival Saturday, and return by train or bus Sunday.

This morning, we change the rest of our money at the bank. I go with Mme. Bougant to see a bicycle agent friend of hers, who promises to take the cycle off my hands on Sunday. Then Morle and I sit on the main square, drink one white wine to our health and our trips—Morle takes some pictures of me getting on the cycle and I am off just at noon.

I immediately take the wrong road and get badly lost— ending up in a swamp full of gypsies—who direct me in English how to get the bicycle through swamp (practically carrying it from stone to stone) and thence to a road, which leads to a road, which leads to the main road to Dinan, my destination tonight.

August 12—St. Brieuc is a very large town—one half quite new and industrial, one half very old, with an old, old square with a public washing place, with many niches and a scrubbing board each for women still working there now, at dinner time, patting round in the wet, their feet protected by wooden shoes. The people everywhere, even the road workers, wear wooden shoes, and the women have on various types of white lace Breton caps. Water is pulled up out of wells with chains turning over a wheel. Children in black pinafores are driving cows along the middle of the road.

August 14—Soon a charming little mademoiselle comes skipping out to offer us the facilities of her house and yard (bicycle storage). She tells me where to buy bread, cheese, lettuce, and tomatoes and suggests we go at 9:00 to the shrine of Notre Dame de Chartes, for the beginning of the Pardon late this evening. We arrive too late to hear the special mass (in the open air—the shrine church itself is very small) and up on a great hill overlooking the sea and the country on all sides. An enormous bonfire is lighted by the candles carried at the head of the procession, and as it burns, the parish priest tells the story of the Pardon in a loud clear voice. He then tells how, in the Thirteenth Century, the fishing fleet went out from Perros Guirec into the worst storm in the memory of the villagers. As the storm increased, the Virgin of Clarte (clear skies) came to the women in the village and told them to light a bonfire on the hill. Meanwhile, the fishermen were praying for deliverance, promising a pardon, as was then the custom throughout Brittany, to any saint who would save them. Suddenly the Virgin of Clarte appeared in a flame and led the fleet back to Perros Guirec.

The Pardon procession included a leader in a navy admiral costume (about the vintage of S. S. Bounty), a bunch of school boys in modern French sailor garb, followed by groups of Brittany peasant women in different white caps and costumes carrying the images from the Rhine. There were eight or ten of these groups—really picturesque. Each group was followed by young school girls singing in red robes. The parade wound down the hill and clear out to the edge of the seashore. Finally the bishop spoke again from the hill top; I went with the crowd through the little flower-filled shrine. I must go back by bus to St. Malo tomorrow at 7:00 a.m.

The bus man puts my bicycle up on top—its last trip with me. I changed busses at St. Brieuc, Dinan Stations. I was not at all sure of finding Petie alive and well when I got back to Madame Bougant's. But I find him robust and sunburned, asleep at three o'clock on Sunday afternoon, trying to catch up rest from a 3:00 a.m. birthday party for Madame Bougant's niece the night before. Later we go the rounds of Morle's pet little street cafes for café au lait and vin blanc. We get the times for trains, and we eat our last dinner at Madame Bougant's—with everyone standing around to deplore our leaving.

San Miguel de Allende,
Helen Miller Bailey 1938

CHAPTER SIX

Since a Family Wasn't Going to Come to Us . . . the Story of the Bailey Boys

"My dad was a drunk and my mother kept us scrubbed hard and beat harder," began the caller, who had introduced himself as Helen Miller Bailey's first legally adopted son, Bruce Morle Bailey. Though eighty-two years old when he first contacted me, Bruce spoke with clarity and easily accessed vivid memories of coming to live with Helen and Morle after escaping an abusive home life.

One afternoon in early 1937, when I was eleven years' old, I'd done something to warrant another whipping. As I sat on the back porch waiting, apparently part of the torture, for Mom to greet me with her whipping stick, something just came over me. I had had enough; there wasn't going to be another beating today. I stood up, jumped off the porch steps and started to run. I ran and ran, as fast as my spindly little legs could carry me, without a destination in mind. I ran until I reached the steps of the Santa Monica police station.

What exactly it was that caused me to start running, I guess I'll never know—self-preservation, divine intervention, animal instinct—but what I do know is that I took charge of my life on that day.

I didn't know exactly what was going to happen at the police station, but I was pretty sure it would not involve being hurt. After considering my situation for about half a minute under the welcoming arch-covered patio entrance, I ventured inside. Maybe it was my answers to their questions or the remnants of my mom's anger still visible on my skinny little body, but next thing I knew I was in a police car headed back to our house. We collected my sister and two brothers and gathered our clothes. Funny, I don't really remember my mom's response. Perhaps she wasn't even there. The cops drove the four of us—the Wall kids—to the Los Angeles Children's Home where people were kind to us. We had enough to eat—everyday. I never did see my mother or father again.

One morning, a few months after we arrived, the home's head mistress approached me at breakfast, "Frank would you like to spend Easter weekend with a nice couple up in the mountains?" I learned these folks were both high school teachers, who had no children of their own. Feeling pretty good about how I had fixed things for myself and the other Wall kids, I was ready for another adventure, "Why not?"

When the pretty, blonde lady and tall, handsome man arrived, the woman handed me a little match box with some holes cut in the top. Inside was a tiny yellow chick. I don't know if I'd ever been given an Easter gift before, but there certainly hasn't been any prize since that I've loved more than that chirping little puff of yellow.

Helen and Morle Bailey drove me to their La Crescenta home, up in the mountains above Los Angeles. I soon learned the Baileys loved animals, especially dogs and horses. I especially liked their little dog, Poochie, a beautiful golden Cocker Spaniel. The place was like Heaven for a kid of 11 from the city. I had a great time; the Baileys were so kind—what a weekend!

A week or so after I had returned to the children's home, the head mistress called me to her office. She explained that the Baileys had really enjoyed my visit. They hoped I would agree to live with them permanently— to be adopted by them. After assurances I would be able to stay in touch with my brothers and sister, I made the second pivotal decision of my life.

As soon as I was settled in and was ready to start school I asked Helen what name I should use in my new life with her. She said I could pick any name I wanted that would sound nice with Bailey, my new last name. On the first day I started picking up books in the school library.

With the help of the librarian I soon grabbed one about a king named Bruce—that was it. I took Morle as my middle name—Bruce Morle Bailey had left Frank Wall behind.

My brothers Don and Ken and my sister Marie (who later changed her name to Emma Mae) were regular visitors to the Bailey home, where we often rode our horses, Goldie, Paloma, and Pablo. Helen started off making sure "the Wall Kids" stayed in touch regularly; we have all these 70 years since the police took us away from our parents.

Those first few months of country living were exhilarating; but, the real excitement started the following summer when Helen and Morle took me on the trip of my life. We went all through Mexico in those three months. My new parents had spent the last three summers there with local guides but this year, feeling quite experienced, perhaps also due to their meager travel budget and the additional expense of a third Bailey, they decided to set their own course.

In Vera Cruz we contracted a small, and very overloaded schooner under sail, the Elena, for the three-day trip across the southern end of the Gulf of Mexico to Merida. Our "captain" hadn't planned on foul weather— man did it come! The little boat tossed and heaved, so did its passengers. Even if we had known which way to head, the storm was in total control. We were stranded on the Elena for seven days. By the fourth day we had run out of food and water. I really thought we were going to die. Luckily, the storm died first and we made it to our destination. We had a much quieter return trip on a much larger sail boat called the Patria. For a twelve-year-old boy, who had never been out of Los Angeles County, this was an unforgettable adventure.

Perhaps that Mexico experience had been a little much even for world travelers Helen and Morle, so the next summer we headed out in our 1935 Ford sedan with a homemade plywood camper shell on top. We drove for three straight months—the entire summer. We saw 44 of the 48 states, two Wonders of the World, and the eastern half of Canada. An older boy named Alfred Campa, who was living with us at the time, accompanied us on the road trip. A former student of Helen's at Manuel Arts High School, he was then attending junior college in Glendale. In fact, Al did most of the driving on that trip.

I remember we were high up on a narrow road coming out of Yellowstone National Park when we felt a wheel come loose. Al barely managed to keep that old jalopy on the road. That was scary, but Yellowstone had been full of surprises. One night, with our little party sound asleep on the ground in their sleeping bags, I awoke with a fright. Our lantern lit up our campsite just enough for me to see a bear who had awakened me by stepping right in the middle of my belly! Oh, I had so many stories to tell when school started up again in the fall.

I graduated from Verdugo Hills High School and joined the United States Navy in 1943.

Regular telephone conversations with the thirty-year Navy veteran were interrupted by a stroke Bruce suffered in 2009. Just before he became ill, Bruce entrusted a painting to me. The large oil willed him by Helen, invites the viewer to one of Bruce's favorite

Mexican towns visited on that trip in 1938—San Miguel de Allende. Sometime after 1955, Helen recreated the piece for a Christmas card inserting herself in the foreground at an easel beside Morle in his wheelchair.

With Bruce off to war . . .

Within the next nine years, Helen and Morle adopted two more boys: Theodore Robert Bailey (Ted) in 1941 at age eleven and, Donald Bailey at age ten in 1945. Captioned family photos list other young men also living with the Baileys. One caption reads, "The two younger boys—Don and Ted just after the big boys came home from the war in 1945." A similar photo is captioned, "Boys living in our house in La Crescenta during first Christmas after the war—1946— Terry Tobin, Bill Hollier, Richard Cardoza, Ted, and Don."

Not for Want of Love . . .

The discovery of why it was that Helen and Morle never had children of their own emerged in part from the recollections of retired ELAC history professor Joel Busch, who Helen had hired in 1972. Professor Busch described a physical characteristic of Helen's not offered by other interviewees, but acknowledged by all once mentioned.

I don't know if you remember that she walked with a kind of swish. Helen would often sit in on my classes when I was first hired on a temporary basis. I never resented her presence, as one might suspect an observation by the department chair might have been considered intrusive in other, less supportive academic settings. Between that smile and the way her sort of sideways gait made her appear to float into the room, she was never a threat, always a welcomed visitor.

For me it was a joy to be in Helen's presence for these reasons: Aside from her strikingly good looks, she had a touch of class, the natural kind that has nothing to do with class consciousness and everything to do with decency, intelligence, broad knowledge and a love of mankind.

Curiosity about Joel's description and my own memory of Helen's unique stride was satisfied in a conversation with Helen's granddaughter, Mary Alice Bailey Welday (herself a teacher/reading specialist). We both knew that Helen's father, Guy Miller had been a prominent dairy farmer in Modesto, California. Although prior interviewees had conjectured that, like Morle, Helen had been stricken with polio, Mary confirmed that as a physically playful young girl, Helen suffered pelvic injuries when she fell to the ground from the barn's hayloft. Reportedly, due to family religious beliefs, Guy and wife Maude rejected proper medical care, which resulted in Helen's limp and her inability to bear children. Regardless the cause, the sidewinding gait plus the long Mexican peasant skirts, did create a kind of mysterious aura, which added to Helen's fascinating presence—the magic of Helen.

Transracial Adoption

Bailey granddaughters, Mary Alice and Maggie, candidly expressed confusion with the incongruence between what the extended Bailey family looked like and its legal status. "Rita, my sister and I have wondered this for a long time; perhaps you can help us understand. While Grandma Doc and Grandpa Petie made a home for many young men of color, they only legally adopted white boys. Can you help us figure this out?" asked Mary Alice.

After some research I was able to explain that for nonrelative adoptions and foster care, the country maintained, legally and culturally, the concept of "matching" children with their adoptive or foster parents. The underlying belief was that physical resemblance and religious continuity of orphans to new parents would lead to a more natural family unit and mitigate the stigma of being less than the "real thing." However, the overwhelming need for placements actually lead to many transracial adoptions. The US Department of Housing and Urban Development estimates that at least two hundred thousand orphaned or abandoned New York children were sent all over the United States and Canada largely by the Children's Aid Society of New York City. In 1854 in New York City alone some thirty thousand abandoned kids were living alone on the streets. The "orphan trains," as they were called, operated from 1854 until 1929.

Unofficially, many extended families were created and recorded before and after what was claimed to be the first transracial legal adoption in 1948 in the United States.

Federal government agencies eventually began to address the plight of homeless and at-risk children. The 1935 Social Security Act allotted funds to the Department of Labor's new Children's Bureau, although a foster care system in the 1930s and 1940s was still largely run by some one hundred private charitable organizations. Legal concerns related to child endangerment, indentured servitude, and child labor described in Rebecca S. Trammel's spring 2009 article for American University's law school's *The Modern American* explain the history of such practices in Europe and precarious lives of many children in America in the first half of the twentieth century.

During this time Helen and Morle brought Mexican American and Korean children into their home and raised them alongside their legally adopted boys. In their roles as public employees and community leaders, they needed to comply with the social norms of the day, but Helen and Morle had openly pushed *the rules* to the limit.

No major Federal child welfare legislation was to be enacted until 1974, the year before Morle died and the year Helen was diagnosed with cancer.

Mother Goose . . .

The two Bailey Boys who stayed the longest were Richard Cardoza and Yung Chung Kim. How Richard came to be a ward of the Baileys was revealed in chapter 4.

Undocumented accounts of how Kim came to live with the Baileys in the early 1950s are quite dramatic. Two versions are the most often repeated: First, an unnamed GI, who had lived with the Baileys prior to serving in Korea, befriended starving teenager Yung Kim. Stowing the youngster in a duffle bag, he brought Kim to the Baileys, who raised him as their own, seeing Kim through his graduate education at Cal Tech. As the second version goes, the same GI advised the Baileys of a very special Korean boy he had met during the war. The Baileys arranged a student visa, which allowed Kim to come to the United States, live with the Baileys and attend school. A local journalist corroborates the latter version:

"A Mother Goose of Sorts
She's a wonderful Symbol of Mothers' Day"
La Cañada Valley Sun, May 6, 1954

One of the most remarkable mothers in La Cañada or anywhere else, even though she has no children of her own, is Dr. Helen Miller Bailey . . . . This vital woman, whose interests and talents range from oil painting to Latin American affairs, has found time in a busy career of teaching, writing, and world travel to adopt and help raise seven boys and provide a home when it was needed most for many others.

She is a very practical and human symbol of Mother's Day which we will observe this Sunday for she has taken orphans, homeless waifs and boys from broken homes under her wing, cared for them, and then turned them back to society where, almost without exception, they are pursuing useful and rewarding careers.

Helen Bailey and husband Morle, also a teacher in Los Angeles and a co-partner in this wonderful project, decided years ago that if a family wasn't going to come to them, they would go to it. The first homeless boy they took under their roof—back in 1937—was Japanese, Kaino Masamitsu, who had been in one of Morle's classes at Roosevelt High School. Kaino lived with them, was assisted by them in securing an education, and now, a University of Chicago graduate and promising engineer, has a family of his own including two children.

The first of three boys sent them by the Children's Home Society of Los Angeles, in that same year that Kaino arrived, was an 11-year-old ostensibly a guest at their La Crescenta home for the Easter holidays . . . . Two more boys came from the Children's Home Society—one now an engineer with Douglas Aircraft, another in the Navy, one from a broken home, two from her classes at Manual Arts, a third who was simply an older brother who needed help, too, one from the Los Angeles County Bureau of Public Assistance, and another she encountered while helping in Boys' Club work. In this group alone there are now a number of university graduates and careers in physics, business, social work, accounting and commercial art.

Helen and her husband bought an acre of ground in La Cañada and moved here in 1948, building their home while they were living in it. Actually, it's located on La Sierra Way in Earl Canyon, just off upper Palm Drive . . . The home is like a mountain lodge, built of logs from Michigan, and beamed ceiling and huge stone fireplace. Several of their boys helped in the construction and they got some professional assistance on the masonry. This is now home for all the boys—six have lived there at one time and on one occasion 14 of them were reunited for a holiday dinner.

Newest of the boys, with a dramatic story all his own, is 17-year-old Yung Chung Kim from Korea. One of Dr. Bailey's foster sons serving in Korea wrote her about Kim and asked her if she would accept another assignment. There was no hesitation. Kim was born in Seoul and attending second year high school when the war broke out. He and his family had to evacuate the city when it was occupied by the Communists and they wandered, homeless and half starved, in that war-torn country for many months.

When UN forces recaptured Seoul, Kim managed to get a job with the American army as an interpreter even though only 15 years old. He had had two years of English in high school. It was during this time that he told the *sergeant, who took an interest in him, of his hope to go to America as a foreign student. With Dr. Bailey's statement of sponsorship and a letter of acceptance from East Los Angeles Junior College, he was past a major hurdle but there was still endless red tape in government examinations and immigration procedure. But he was prepared for he had not only saved the $40 a month he got from the US Army but had studied at nights during the war so that he was able to pass the difficult tests for a high school diploma. From a select field of 50 awaiting visas to come to America for study, Kim was one of only seven to go. He received a six-year visa and in September of last year found himself in Southern California living with the Baileys.*

Kim and Dr. Bailey commute each day by auto to the junior college where he is a freshman in civil engineering.

Family albums suggest that the foster son serving in Korea was likely Frazier Moore who wrote Helen asking Helen to take on the young Korean boy, who was determined to study engineering and was suffering like many youngsters in that post-war environment. Yung-Chung Kim lived with the Bailey's until he earned his master's degree from Cal Tech in Engineering and PhD from University of Southern California.

Children of adopted sons Don and Ted call him "Uncle Kim." Family photo albums always include Kim and later his wife and children. Dr. Kim retired in 2005 with professor emeritus status from California State University of Los Angeles where he had taught since 1965 and had served as long time chair of the Civil Engineering Department.

Helen and Morle Bailey early 1930s

Santa Monica Police
Station, circa 1930

Children's Home Society,
Los Angeles, CA

Bruce, Helen, Poochie, and Morle Bailey 1937

Wall kids, Marie, Don, Frank, and Ken

Alfred Campa and Helen

Helen, son Ted, Morle and assorted pets, 1945

Older boys (Frazier Moore and Bill Hollier) visiting after the War

Bailey Family Christmas Party 1954

Bridge along the Pan American Highway,

Helen Miller Bailey

CHAPTER SEVEN

A Revolutionary Promise of Rural Education: Mexico 1934–1944

Helen and Morle had honeymooned in Panama in 1932 and returned to Latin America ten times over the following twenty-three years. They spent their first summer in Mexico in 1934 when they drove from Los Angeles to Oaxaca on the newly completed Pan American Highway. Based in large part on these trips, Helen authored (or co-authored) three Latin American textbooks: *Santa Cruz of the Etla Hills* (1955); *Latin America: the Development of Its Civilization* (Bailey and Nasatir 1960); and *The Latin Americans: Past and Present* (Bailey and Cruz 1972).

Helen was initially drawn to investigate Mexico's revolutionary promise of equal distribution of land and free public education. In fact, Mexico's 1917 Constitution exceeded other modern constitutions in defining the state's responsibility to provide education to all by limiting all other plans, programs (parochial schools), and teaching methods not sponsored by the government. The ability to educate all the people was a visionary and an incalculable undertaking since the country then had few teachers (all previously unsupported by the government) with so much to rebuild in the aftermath of a war in which hundreds of thousands of Mexicans had perished. But this was a "grounds up" plan in which the villagers themselves would build the schools and the government would train and provide teachers that would serve as leaders in the new order; Helen provides a detailed description of how a small village implemented the plan in *Santa Cruz of the Etla Hills*. In 1955 "about the author" notes, Helen explains that she came to Mexico to study the sociological details of life as guests of the rural school authorities and was assigned to the Santa Cruz Etla school. She wrote the reason for her return in 1945 was "to work in the campaign against illiteracy."

The government did do its part. Just one year after the new Federal government was elected in 1920, the first administrator of federal education was chartered to staff rural schools in all villages; by 1930, three thousand five hundred schools had been added, making a total of twenty-five thousand elementary schools (a 16 percent increase from 1920). In 2013 UNISEF reported the mixture of Mexico's public and private, urban, and rural primary schools, have achieved a literacy rate among fifteen to twenty-four-year-olds of over 98 percent.

With a similar interest in the progress of education, and seemingly without regard to political unrest or volatile traveling conditions, the Baileys later visited Africa just as several countries were winning their independence from colonial rule. Helen had prearranged visits to several rural schools, "So the summer of 1962 found us set on going all the way 'round Africa to visit the newly created nations now in the UN, to see what hopes and plans they have for educating their masses . . . I am interested in the emerging nations, Morle in the geography, geology and wildlife."

Of the fourteen African countries visited that summer (1962), ten had just recently decolonized: Uganda had become independent that same year; Kenya was in the midst of the process; Tanganyika (Zanzibar) the year before; Senegal, French Congo, French Equatorial Africa, and Nigeria in 1960; Ghana in 1957; and Sudan and Morocco in 1956. Chapter 11 provides a glimpse of that trip as does Helen's film footage available at *http://uschefnerarchive.com/project/baileyfilms/*.

But it was Mexico where Helen would focus her energy and academic interests. During her many visits to Oaxaca, Helen worked with locals to set up a school and secure medical services for the hill town community. She became very close to one family and supported their daughter through nursing school in Mexico City. In notes to South Florida University Press (publisher of *Santa Cruz Etla*), Helen refers to eleven summers spent in Mexico, Central America and South America between 1933 and 1954. And in an almost apologetic explanation of her ongoing support of nursing school expenses, Helen wrote,

> *Sixty pesos a month was then less than five dollars. At East Los Angeles Junior College I was teaching a class of young would-be social workers, most themselves of Mexican ancestry, sending them out to do practice work in boys' clubs and social centers. The children they work with were sometimes but one generation removed from the Santa Cruz Etlas of many parts of Mexico.*
>
> *I have talked a great deal about my service to the Los Angeles under-privileged community, but the actual truth*

is that I got more than five dollars an hour extra for the four hours a week I put in supervising the social-work students in the evenings. How could my conscience rest easy, when Margarita could go to secondary school a whole month with only one of these easily earned five-dollar bills? . . . If any of the hundreds of my own splendid students of Mexican ancestry in East Los Angeles who heard about this wondered why I was sending money down to Mexico every month from 1954 to 1956, when the need for funds for medical education is just as great among them, I could only answer sadly: Find me a way that I can send a Los Angeles city student of Mexican ancestry through any American medical school at a total of five dollars a month, and I will surely do it."

Helen's "1944 Mitla" travel journal suggests her forthcoming book about an Oaxaca hill town, albeit a decade later:

I sit down to write again in the hotel in Oaxaca. The visit to Santa Cruz Etla was the high point of several trips (to Mexico since 1934) and would justify our coming all this way, if for nothing else than the peace of mind I get from being among such happy, peaceful, friendly, contented people. If ever I were to write anything worthwhile for adults, it would probably be about that community, our village, where I myself am now called Doña Elena (Helen), and am very much one of the family.

Santa Cruz Etla is really on three ridges. Up the center one runs the ox cart road, the brook from the higher hills is canalized to run down the top of the ridge and in a level cleared place is the school, the municipal building and the foundations of a church (which men of the community started to build since we were here last, and had to quit because of the high price of cement.) Most families live in adobe huts, with little cleared places for the cattle to be tethered. The fields farmed by the families stretch down on either side of the ridge. From every house in Santa Cruz Etla there is a breath-taking view.

On up, the hills are covered with heavy woods, woods which are considered in community holding to all the people, and where the young men go to cut firewood for sale in Oaxaca for a cash income. The older men plow the land with oxen, planting corn and beans in the rainy season and harvesting in the dry. Each family has about two and a half acres of land and grows enough so that few ever have to buy food. The little gardens around the houses produce mangoes, avocadoes and squash, and chickens, turkeys, and young pigs provide occasional meat for fiestas.

Their houses are bare inside, with earth floor, and no windows, and only an occasional crudely made table or bench. Children go to school through the 4th grade (ambitious boys can go to the 5th and 6th at San Pablo— only six in town are now doing so) then share in the work—girls marry at 15 or 16, boys at 20 or 21.

The town is governed by a municipal committee chosen every year, and there are so many offices that everyone gets a turn at something, whether he can read or write or not. Here in Santa Cruz they are all people of great dignity and importance, and call each other by their first names with the title of Don or Doña attached. On Saturdays they take firewood and farm products to market to get money to buy cloth for clothes, guarache sandals, pottery dishes and their few other needs. There in the market of Oaxaca they are suddenly poor ragged Indians, undistinguishable from all the other ragged Indians of Mexico. Yet in Santa Cruz Elta they are the happiest people I have ever known.

Quickly the word passed around that Doña Elena had come again to Santa Cruz, with another "hueriano" (an orphan boy—Bruce was there in 1938) to draw, to photograph, to write, and to talk with them.

We find changes and improvements in the families. Don Martin now bakes bread, small brown wheat loaves, for the villagers to intersperse with tortillas; Don Julio has a mill to grind his own corn; Don Esteban now the mayor, has organized the building of a cemetery ("pantheon") beyond the ridge so the dead "angelitos" of Santa Cruz no longer need to be sent to San Pablo for burial.

I ask them about the history of the community and we piece together a story which they learned from their fathers . . . Carlos IV King of Spain (1788 to 1808) gave Mixtecan and Zapotecan Indian communities of the mountains and foothills of Oaxaca Valley independent charters to own and cultivate land. Such a community was Santa Cruz Salinas two ridges away. After the "wars against the French" (Maximilian self-proclaimed Emperor of Mexico in 1864), Don Amado's grandfather came home to find the town had a great cholera epidemic—only a few families were left. Those of the northern ridge of Santa Cruz Salinas came two ridges over to the upper foothills; those of the lower ridge went below to San Pablo Etla.

They moved to leave the "poisoned ground" and houses where the cholera had been.

We take a bus to Mitla where we find a very nice rural school, occupying six rooms of the 3-sided arcade which makes the municipal building on one side and the market on the other. I'm intrigued with this 5th grade— "Mitla's highest class" the children told me—four boys and two girls—and suddenly an idea strikes me—why not get to know these six children very well—their school life, their home life—then take many photographs of them, and write them up for a 5th or 6th or 7th grade reader (they are all 13 years old.)

I find their homes represent a travelling muleteer or trader, a town official, a tenant farmer, a permanent market booth holder, a road worker on the international highway, and a guard at the ruins—The story of their lives would describe many a Mexican town. The Senorita, having been given my letter from the Director telling her to "do everything to make my happy," is enthusiastic about the idea, and sells it to the fifth graders. Therefore, the great part of my remaining stay in Mitla will be concerned with the lives of Abel, Adolfo, Enerdino, Petra, Lupe, and Samuel, and there will be little time to write more than copious notes I will have to take on their lives and their conversation with me.

My schedule is altered by visiting the children's homes on Saturday and going to the market town of Tlacolula for the big Sunday market. The first mother was president of the League of Mothers (all who speak Spanish and read and write). She is a Tehuana and has on the square embroidered blouse, if not the white frilly headdress of the women of

Tehuantepec. Her husband is a trader for coffee beans from the more tropical towns to the south, taking manufactured articles from Oaxaca City out on burros, and returning every two weeks or so. Adolfo, my fifth grader, is the only son of this prosperous trader and will be sent on to 6th grade in Tlacolula or Oaxaca as his mother feels that a better educated trader makes better trading deals.

Samuel and his father are at work pulling weeds along the crumbled edge of the sacrificial court. The friendly father tells me he doesn't want Samuel to be a gardener at the ruins, but to be a teacher like his older brother. He sends Samuel with me to the poor thatch and cactus home yard where I get many pictures of the family. His mother tells me how the family sacrificed to send the elder boy not only to the 6th grade, but on through five years more of the Instituto in Oaxaca so he could be a rural teacher.

Enerdino's mother and father both work in the fields on Saturday plowing the corn with oxen because the father as "Chief of Police" (or head of the night guard which patrols the town) is so busy this year on other days attending Council meetings, that his fields are neglected. Enerdino comes back to get me after lunch and takes me to his two room adobe . . . the father speaks very good Spanish, although the grandparents I photographed know only Zapotecan. I am regaled with orange pop, tacos, and questions about life in the United States ("United States" is just another town to them). They certainly are not conscious about the war[WWII], although five young men, one a cousin of Enerdino, have been conscripted for a year's training. They are surprised that some Americans have been killed, and ask if any airplanes "have fallen." As I leave Enerdino's father asks me, "Why is your tierra fighting the war?"

Their teacher has also arranged for Petra (the one regular girl member of the class) to take me to visit wool workers, carders, spinners, and weavers. The people here no longer make the Indian wool skirts for women (but wear tightly wrapped dark or plaid cotton ones)—so weavers now only make the wide red and rose colored belts (8 inches) which every woman in this end of the valley wears wrapped many times around the waist. Carding is done with Spanish carding "paddles," and spinning on the Guatemalan fashion, with a sharp pointed stick or spindle twirled in a saucer. A young man does the weaving and stands up to hold the loom tight, bracing against a tree. Petra does not want to be a weaver because "it is much easier to buy cotton cloth in bright colors, ready to sew." We also watch a felt sombrero maker, who takes piles of carded white wool, works it inside wet sacking over a metal plate heated by charcoal, until after two days he has a stiff gray felt "Stetson" to sell for 7 pesos. (Factory made hats are also putting him out of business.) This is a felt hat-wearing, not a straw-sombrero-wearing town. We also watch maguey fibre (with the maguey juice and most distilled out for tequila) being soaked in the river and twisted up into rope—a major town product.

I learned more about the village from reading "Mitla, Town of Souls" by Elsie Clews Parsons, a University of Chicago student who lived in our inn in Mitla for three years and investigated Indian customs which are a holdover from the days before the conquest.

Notes: I spent all day Friday and Saturday morning answering letters from students and Manual Arts boys who were in the service.

Mitla (an important archeological site) comes from Nahuati, the language of the Aztecs and derived from Michtlan "place of the dear." The Zapotec name was Lyobaa which means place of rest.

Shortened Summer 1944 Travel Schedule

This summer, after three summers spent sitting at home in La Crescenta writing a text book, we are determined, war or no war, to get back to Mexico. We will have only eight weeks as I have promised to work a week for the Red Cross after I come back and have worked now since school was out. So we are ready to go July 1 but have to wait for wartime train reservations to Tucson, Arizona, until July 3. Even then we stand in a crowd . . . Mexican workers have come into the United States by the thousands for agricultural war time work . . .

World Travelling as Teachers in 1944—Perhaps not as Romantic as Might Be Thought

Our only great tragedy at Mazatlan was the bugs of the bay. Fleas we have always had on any travels; lice and bedbugs we encountered in Ireland. But not only were the familiar flat brown bedbugs here in abundance, but a new and strange thing by the hundreds—a tiny clear white thing 1/16 of an inch across, which turns bright red as soon as it gets blood in it. The double bed in the room had an old mattress filled with these and bedbugs. The small things sting and burn and produce swellings.

The first night Morle had a canvas cot near the window while Teddy and I slept on the double bed. Tired as I was the bugs drove me on to the floor by midnight, but Teddy stayed on, and had his eyes swollen shut and his face covered with scores by morning . . . We forgot the bugs in the glory of the last night on the beach and the most beautiful rainbow I ever remember seeing.

Visiting Old Friends

In Oaxaca, we want to first find Rosita, the pretty little Mexican teacher who was in the rural school at Santa Cruz Etla where we lived in the summer of 1934, who came to visit the schools of Los Angeles on an international exchange in 1937, and who was afterwards sent to organize a kindergarten in the Indian village of Mitla 20 miles out of Oaxaca at the ruins. Although one of our best friends of all time, we have lost track of her because of the difficulty of letter writing in two languages. If we could find her we could again visit Santa Cruz Etla to see the progress the school has brought to the village . . . We hope my letter to the Education Director will open the door to all these plans and help us find her.

Ancient Zapotec Jewelry in Oaxaca City from Mitla

. . . we are urged to see the new museum on the park where all the gold, jade and coral ornaments, taken from the tombs at Monte Alban are now on display . . . Here are beautifully worked gold jewelry, enameled pottery, carved turquoise, and the skeletons of the 9 priests or kings, who were buried in all this finery somewhere about 12 or 1300 A.D. across the valley from their city of Mitla. These beautiful things were found in 1927 by Mexican archeologists and were sent to the Chicago World's Fair. (Now returned to) the modern town built by the descendants of the Zapotecans who made them. As far as detailed hand work is concerned, they constitute the richest find in the history of American Indian Archeology.

Free France /Bastille Day Parade

I went to the Secretariat of Education for all Mexico, presented my credentials, reminded the officer of my visit to Oaxaca before, and secured letters of introduction to the Director of Education for the state of Oaxaca. On the way back to the Eastman Kodak Company, Mexican branch, I suddenly found myself in a parade of soldiers, society women, school children, and Mexican Boy scouts, all carrying banners and pushing floats in honor of Free France, and Bastille Day July 14. The banners urged France to become again a free nation—that was the wish of her sister Mexico.

One group of young girls . . . were singing the
Marseillaise, and as they passed, the crowd in the sidewalk
began singing also. So there I stood lifting up my voice,
"allous enfants de la Patrie, le jour de gloire est arrive,"
with a lump in my throat for war torn France.

Christening of Vivianna Marta in Mexico City

We were anxious to get on to Mexico City to see
Ricardo Garcia Mercado old friend and former student.
He had left Los Angeles at 15 in the 10th grade in 1932 to
come back to Mexico and we had found him our guide and
guardian angel and interpreter in 1933, our first summer
in Mexico. We have always found him here on trips since,
and now he has married, and has two little girls. He came
to Los Angeles in April this year to see about further art
training and spent Easter vacation with us. Urging us to
come to Mexico this summer and be the god parents at
the christening of his second baby, a serious procedure
in Mexico, which ties the god parents to the family in
an almost blood relation. We are honored to have been
asked, and hope that the telegram explaining our delay,
in Mazatlan and Guadalajara, have reached him.

The crowd filled the tiny house . . . To all these people
Ricardo's wife, Tella, and her tireless little mother, served
chicken cooked in the thick red hot chili sauce called
"mole." They had cooked three chickens, and ground up
enough chilies to make a clay tub full of mole (sauce).
There were no spoons and we were supposed to tear off
pieces of tortilla and dip them into the sauce to scoop up

the chicken. I ate six large tortillas worth. The only other things served were Spanish fried rice, a small plate a piece, beans, and beer.

On the spur of the moment we had worked out a plan for his second son Armand (called Chaco) to come to Los Angeles in September. . . going back and forth to Americanization classes with me, he could get a year of English. He planned to arrive September 1, a few days after we get home.

(The next morning) We needed a wedge hammer to put us on that train—the rapid train to Guadalajara and on to Mazatlan. Morle forced a way through towards the center of the car with his crutches, and there we stood, Morle held up by one crutch, I by the other, and Teddy suspended almost in midair by the packed crowd. We could hardly see out the window to wave goodbye to all the friends who had come to wish us Godspeed.

Near us on the train sat a Mexican gentleman born in Los Angeles, who spoke very good English and taught English in the Mazatlan secondary schools. His wife was ill in Guadalajara, his mother and children were with her, his servants were on vacation. He was going home to an empty house. Wouldn't we come and stay our week in Mazatlan with him?

It sounded too good to be true . . . His house was on the north beach side far out from the center. Inside it was hot and stuffy but there were many rooms around a patio. It was very thick with dust and spiders, no one had cleaned it since his wife was taken sick two months before. The gentleman brought in our suit cases and then asked us about breakfast. Now the truth came out. In all good faith and spirit he had "adopted" a transient family which had a mother of the family in it to clean the house, do the marketing and the cooking.

I was appalled, but meant to be game. (After a walk to the city market a mile or more on the other side of town) I began to long for the inn we had paid eleven pesos a day for its bed-buggy room, three meals a piece and our privacy.

(In the morning) I found Morle awake and troubled. It was so hot he couldn't sleep. The house backed up against a cliff and there was no breeze at all in the little pocket of a street. It fronted on a slough where mosquitoes bred and the house was full of them. He was thinking about the cool breeze in the open upstairs rooms of the inn, "If it weren't for you, wanting to cook things you like here, I'd ditch the gentleman right now and go to the inn." Well to make a long story short, while the man was still sleeping, Morle and I went out and hired a little horse drawn taxi and hit it for the inn. The people were delighted to see us; the most open breezy room full of canvas cots was unoccupied. I stayed to hold the room. Morle and the taxi driver picked up Teddy on the beach, drove back to the house to get the suit cases.

In his explanation to the gentleman he could blame everything on me. I had refused to market and cook Mexican style—and what could you do with a woman like that. The gentleman thought American woman were given too much freedom.

Now the inn seemed luxurious. We stayed seven days and did not see any bugs, fleas or mosquitoes. Every morning at 5:00 children Teddy's age in the house waked us and he and I went with them to swim till 7:00. After breakfast I would write all morning while Morle sat on our balcony and looked out through the new telescope he had bought in the pawn shop in Mexico City. In the afternoon it often clouded over and was less hot so that Morle and Teddy would go out with me to sketch the pink houses and Coco palm trees.

It was like life on a tropical south sea isle. I finished my Mitla story, Morle mounted the photos for me in a scrapbook, Teddy fished off the pier—when we were called to meals we went. The palm trees, the sunsets, the islands (Teddy and I climbed way up a hill to get shots of the whole town and bay one hot morning—hope the censor let them by) will make some Kodachromes. Soldiers stopped me from taking pictures of the port, saying drawings or pictures of the hills, the sea, the docks, etc. would be censored.

Post Script: the return trip—Mazatlan to Los Angeles

(We encountered the) greatest heat wave of the summer, hitting Mazatlan . . . and following us all the way into Los Angeles. No seats in second-class car when we got on—Morle sat three deep with baby children and suitcases in a shared seat, I sat on the arm of seat already occupied by three peons, Ted sat on our suitcases on the floor. The bridge washed out 2-1/2 hours out of Mazatlan (we had then been on the crowded train in the stifling heat for four hours.) The train was warned of the wash-out in time to stop, but stayed there in the coastal underbrush

jungle, waiting for repairs for eight hours—no food, nor water on the train.

Next day, already 12 hours into Ciudad Obregon, our second-class car broke a wheel. Our car was abandoned, everyone, including pet parrots were shoved into the other cars, onto the steps of the cars, and even onto the engine tender, as there were no spare passenger cars of any kind in Ciudad Obregon. Through-passengers to the border, still 18 hours away, were shoved into first class, much to the disgust of the "upper-class" Mexican already there, who had paid twice the fare to be in the cleaner, less crowded plush-seated car.

(Note: The one Pullman car, carrying eight American tourists, who had paid four times the second-class fare, was not in any way disturbed—in fact the hermetically-sealed passengers never knew what happened.)

We passed without the slightest difficulty at the border, not being asked to show any films or manuscript. Morle and I even got seats on the train in Tucson, while Teddy was taken in as a pal by a car full of soldiers and sailors. So (we're on our way) home with ten dollars to spare in our pockets, and two more aftermaths, one good—all the Kodachromes were returned within six weeks, none censored, few spoiled, and many beautiful; and one bad aftermath—Armando, Ricardo's brother-in-law, was refused an entry permit to the U.S. until his sixteenth birthday in May, so never left Mexico City. He will be with us next year, then, instead—a short postponement as things go in Mexico.

Helen and Henry Morle Bailey in Mexico, 1934

East Los Angeles College campus site sketched from
Brooklyn Avenue in 1947, Helen Miller Bailey

CHAPTER EIGHT

Blazing the Trail from Hicks Camp to College

Mayor Gutiérrez was officiating at an event on a miserably hot August day in 2005. I made the best of the delay by viewing the treasures of the tiny *La Historia Museo de Los Barrios* in El Monte, California, where my interview with the city's mayor was scheduled. I browsed through photos and artifacts from the nine "pickers' camps," which had served as makeshift homes for migrant Mexican agricultural workers and their families in the 1930s and 1940s in California's San Gabriel Valley. First open to the public on September 29, 2001, the little museum's collection includes artifacts, photos, and letters to and from camps *Canta Ranas*, Chino, Wiggins, *Las Flores*, *Granada*, *La Misión*, Hicks, and *La Sección*. Several of the elderly docents who greeted me that morning had grown up in Hicks Camp (named for the farmer who owned the land).

After taking in all the contents of the permanent exhibits, I sat down at a small round plastic table with four docents who had invited me for coffee, while I waited for the mayor. The docents explained their mission to document the Mexican and Native American heritage of the area and described a brewing controversy. They were insistent that the City of El Monte grant them space within the city hall's museum which was dedicated to commemorating the "pioneers" from Oklahoma who had "settled" the area.

However, from pottery samples, archeologists place the *Tongva* peoples in the Los Angeles Basin and Channel Islands area up to eleven thousand years ago. The *Tongva* (known today as the *Gabrielinos*, after the Mission San Gabriel), were one of the twenty-two linguistic families of Native Americans. In 1914 the nine-thousand-year-old skeleton of a *Tongva* woman was unearthed from the La Brea Tar Pits in Los Angeles.

Nearly two hundred years after European exploration in 1592, Spanish Franciscan missionaries founded the nearby San Gabriel Archangel Mission in 1771. The area was Mexican territory, thus Mexican families had lived in the area long before the "Okies" who arrived in small numbers after the end of the Mexican American War, which resulted in the United States paying Mexico $18 million for California in 1840. In the late 1930s, they were followed by other Oklahomans escaping the dust bowl conditions of their overused and indebted farms.

Ernie Gutiérrez, El Monte's mayor, is one of many success stories out of Hicks Camp. As I listened to the docents, I guessed he must walk a fine line between his insistent *compadres* and the revisionist historians, descendants of those Oklahoma families, who were also his important constituents. With history on their side, and 70 percent of current El Monte residents Mexican American, the logical conclusion would be that the founders of *La Historia Museo* would see their dream of historical recognition realized. While the small plot of land on which their precious artifacts and memories are preserved was donated by the City of El Monte, official support apparently ended there.

Prejudice is not logical or rational. The hypocrisy that perpetuates it is more covert today, but no less sinister and pervasive, even in the most civil societies in the twenty-first century.

The celebration of indigenous people and reverence for Mexican American heritage is confined to the tiny fifteen-by-thirty-foot building, while the more recent timeline of white settlement is enshrined in the modern El Monte Historical Museum adjacent to the official center of the City of El Monte. The deep seated bias against which Helen dedicated her life was thrust into the open within this, the first hour of my research of Doc Bailey's life.

The docents' recollections of days gone by in the camps soon focused on Father John Coffield, the Catholic priest whose parish was Hicks Camp. Docent Richard Perez was a tall, dark-skinned man of about eighty, who I guessed had been a very handsome young man. He spoke with joy, and a couple missing teeth, about the camp's Boy Scout troop and its leader, Father Coffield:

> *We were too poor to have uniforms and badges and no one's house was big enough for our meetings, but Father had a way of making us feel like we were official; after all, we had a troop number and everything. Once a month or so, depending on where our parents were picking (the docents explained that Hicks Camp families started with*

grapes and graduated to onions and then walnuts), Father
would load as many troop members as he could into his
old station wagon and take us to the beach, sometimes a
baseball game, and several times to my favorite place,
a cabin up in the mountains not too far from here. A
beautiful blonde lady lived in that cabin and she let us and
other rag tag-troops camp on her land.

I started to squirm a bit in my plastic folding chair. It couldn't be, could it, that Dr. Bailey was the woman Richard was talking about? I had just recently learned that Helen had worked with Father Coffield; indeed, the journalist who had written the story of the influential priest's passing in February 2005 had mentioned Helen in the obituary. When telephoned about his *San Gabriel Tribune* article, Jason Kosareff elaborated on the unlikely pair's efforts on behalf of young Latinos—an "underground railroad of sorts," he labeled their work. He explained that in the early days of East Los Angeles College the children of migrant workers were not allowed to enroll.

To right this injustice, Father Coffield would identify high-potential young men from Hicks Camp and Helen would use her influence as the social sciences department chair to enroll pickers' sons, find them places to live near campus, jobs, and scholarships to ensure they could focus on their studies. Jason had encouraged my visit to *La Historia Museo* to speak with its founders for more information about Helen Miller Bailey.

Richard smiled and leaned back from the small round table, "We all slept on the land around the cabin in little tents. Sometimes there were as many as two hundred of us from all over Los Angeles. It was so exciting! In the morning, the pretty lady would come out of her log house, heat up a large grill and make us pancakes and scrambled eggs. She wasn't a very good cook, but her beautiful smile and blonde hair were captivating."

The suspense was too much. I excused myself and hurried out to my car to retrieve a copy of Dr. Bailey's text, *Santa Cruz of the Etla Hills* which included photos of Helen in Mexico, which might confirm my suspicion. I flipped through the pages to the largest photo of Helen and raced back inside the tiny museum to the little coffee klatch. I interrupted the group by placing the opened book on the plastic table. Richard reacted instantly and emotionally,

"That's her—that's the lady," he said with tears welling up in his beautiful brown eyes. "How did you know?" He didn't look up from the book. "I told you she was beautiful." Richard pined as he passed the book to his curious peers around the table.

Years later when Helen's granddaughter, Mary Alice, and I connected, she confirmed that cooking was not high on Helen's priority list. Richard's recollection was correct; Helen wasn't much of a cook. But if it meant these boys could enjoy a weekend without care or struggle, evidently, she'd even flip pancakes.

Mary Alice recalled her grandmother's focus away from domestic activities and toward a very modern lifestyle for a woman in the mid-1900s—swimming and reading the newspaper every morning before driving off to campus, lecturing to civic groups, initiating political discussions among the family. Although Mary Alice added that Grandma Doc "still took the time to make me feel special, capable, and loved." Mary attributes her ability to complete her college work and her drive to become a teacher to the encouragement and guidance from her grandmother.

Although Mayor Gutiérrez had been detained for quite a while at the park ceremony, I didn't mind a bit. I was learning things about

Helen that no newspaper articles or proclamations could convey. That morning, Richard exhibited feelings that were to be repeated many times in subsequent interviews with Helen's contemporaries. He was the first of many to reveal how the mere sight of Helen evoked the same dreamy, sweet memories. Helen's smile, a bit flirtatious, definitely comforting, combined with that mouthful of perfectly straight white teeth, worked like a sandwich board sign reading, "I genuinely care about you. I can be anything you want me to be—your *abuelita* (grandmother), your mentor, your inspiration, or simply, your teacher. More importantly, you can be anything you want to be."

Youngsters from Hicks Camp rose to Father Coffield's and Helen's expectations. One of the more compelling stories is that of Dr. Ben Campos, whom some say is the first person in El Monte, California, to earn a PhD degree.

Campos recalls Father Coffield and Ramona Sanchez of the Catholic Youth Organization in Hicks Camp driving him to meet Helen in 1952. The college professor walked him through the registration process at East Los Angeles College and became a friend and counselor. In fact five young men from Hicks, including Mayor Ernie Gutiérrez, had been selected at the same time to be enrolled in college—that was out of the three hundred families who lived in Hicks Camp, the largest in the San Gabriel Valley. At the same time dozens of veterans of the Korean Conflict were also entering the college.

During his two years at ELAC, Campos served as a reader for Helen's *Santa Cruz Etla* and helped her with the Spanish. He recalls a busy two years at East Los Angeles College:

In those years at ELAC Doc would take our group from the Sociology and Spanish Clubs to talk to high school students and encourage them. We did it a lot. At Roosevelt High we met Mr. Bailey. The Baileys took us to Balboa Island and to several national parks. On these trips Mr. Bailey taught us how to use a fork instead of a tortilla. At her mountain home, Helen fed us meatloaf—we couldn't get enough and she encouraged us. I remember her son Don, saying, "Man, leave him alone—he's had enough!"

Being in their presence provided many lessons. Mr. Bailey had a quiet confidence about him. He seemed very wise. And Helen's demeanor was always so professional around her colleagues. As a couple, they seemed very used to each other.

Helen delivered Ben Campos' degree from East Los Angeles College to his home in Hicks Camp and met his grandmother who could not attend the graduation ceremony. Campos remembers being amazed that she drove alone all the way through the camp's dirt road, riddled with potholes. "When I look back now, I see that she was a teacher who instructed through her actions, just as much, if not more, as through her lectures."

Campos enlisted in the US Army in 1955 for a two-year stint after completing his studies at ELAC. Upon returning home, he enrolled at Cal State Los Angeles, having submitted his application while still in the service and stationed in Germany. He earned a bachelor's degree in education there in 1960, all the while working in various schools and playground programs. He was hired as a Spanish teacher for the El Monte School District and travelled to many schools for about two years. In 1964 he was recruited to lead the first Head Start program in the area. He visited homes, walking the area, and helping parents understand the benefits to their children. He spent the next three decades working for federal programs such as Title I high school migrant education. Dr. Campos earned his doctoral degree in education in 1982 from University of Southern California.

Father Coffield was honored with a lifetime membership in the California Teachers' Association for his role in the desegregation of El Monte schools. The priest expressed his feelings for his fellow human rights advocate in a letter at the end of her four-decade teaching career.

OUR LADY OF GUADALUPE CHURCH

544 E. Central Avenue

Santa Ana, California 92707

Telephone: 545-5434

Dear Helen,

Benny Campos and Martin Alfaro were pioneers out of Hicks Camp. Behind them was the carping that they couldn't make it. It wasn't any use, they would have to go back to work in the fields. What were they doing acting like gringos? Ahead of them, a fearful hurdle of Junior College, a strange and fearful world.

They had the good fortune to go to East Los Angeles Junior College and the great blessing to be within the realm of influence of a giant of a person, so very rare in those days, a person who had a vision of the potential that lay within those shy personalities of our Mexican American brothers.

So often I thank the Father of All for having a daughter like you, who could communicate his trust and caring and love to the more neglected of his children who found it hard to believe in themselves. I love you and salute you.

Gratefully,

Juanote (del Monte)

Father John V. Coffield

Helen Miller Bailey

Unknown Hill Town and Church,

Helen Miller Bailey

CHAPTER NINE
A Life Defined: Before and After Macchu Picchu, 1947 Journal Excerpts

This year we must see South America, part of it at least—so I have chosen the west coast countries of Ecuador and Peru because of my great interest in the Incas and the archeological remains of their history. We are taking an eleven-year-old orphan boy, Donald Lee Graves, a ward of the County, who makes his home with us. ["Donny" would later be adopted by the Baileys.] The plan is to start at Quito, visit Indian towns and ruins en route to Guayaquil, taking two or three weeks, sketching and photographing. Morle will stay in Guayaquil or some nearby fishing village, while Donny and I go on down the Pan American Highway into Peru. We will go up into the Andes visiting ruins as far as Lake Titicacca, and return to Morle, planning to be away about three weeks. Via second class busses we'll travel from Quito to Bogota and hope to take the river steamers down to Cartagena and Barranquilla, where we will catch our Panama-Balboa return trip home by August 31.

Traveling Light

Our equipment includes, besides the two cameras and all the film, paints and paper, which almost fills one suitcase, two complete outfits of "roughing it" clothes for each of us (seersucker for me, jeans for Donny, open-collar easy wash shirts for Morle), a coat and sweater for each, one change of underwear a piece, and a first-aid kit. (Additionally), we had gone to such difficulty and trouble at home getting visas on these countries, all of them requiring health certificates, vaccination certificates, letters from our bankers, marriage license, clearance of police record, as well as permission and passport clearance to take Donny with us.

We remembered Panama City and the Zone with great pleasure from a summer spent there in 1932 (honeymooning), so knew our way around and went to look at old landmarks. There have been some changes, (although) we were distressed to see discrimination against Negroes still very much in evidence in the markets, quarters, drinking fountains, etc., of the Zone, even at the international airport, from where we caught another flight to Quito, Peru.

It isn't that we didn't like Quito—it is picturesque, many places to hike and visit, poncho-clad Indians running through the streets, Indian markets three days a week, but we had three things against it: It rained all the time, the average temperature in the daytime was that of a cold Los Angeles rainy winter day, and the nights much colder, and of course the 9,500 feet altitude.

A Black Market for Green

One reason we have a hard time planning any budget is the terrific difference in legal exchange (sol to dollar) and the black market exchange in Peru. The banks will only give the "government" price of six sols to the dollar—while a man in Tumbes gave me 11.50 in the hotel there, the bus agent in Trujillo gave me ten and the hotel in Lima, twelve.

Six different ridges of the Andes, on a train, a bus, and three trucks from Lima to Cuzco

As we went up to the snow line and down into the valley all over again I kept asking why, with Abancay a state capital and a larger town than many others, there wouldn't be "through traffic" all day— but the drivers laughed it off—no one ever made two of these laps in one day . . . It was so hot, that when our driver left us at a little rooming house where there was a shower, I washed my hair and took a bath and washed out a lot of clothes under the shower.

[Then] came a knock at the door, and there was another truck driver, friend of ours, who had told this new driver about us. Did we want to go to Cuzco? When would he leave in the morning—very early we hoped—"I am not going in the morning, Senora, I am going now." Impossible! To get to Cuzco yet today! Why not—before midnight anyway.

Unbelievable as it seemed, we really were gone out of Abancay within a half hour, clutching rolls and chunks of fried meat hurriedly purchased while the truck driver cleared his load with the state authorities. In this truck we both sat on a bench built into the wooden truck body behind the driver. We roused the landlady at our boarding

159

house in Cuzco at 12:30 a.m. We went wearily to sleep having arrived in Cuzco, five days' travel from Lima to cover 600 miles, over six different ridges of the Andes, on a train, a bus, and three trucks. But Bolivar and Pizarro both took an army through the same route when the Pan American Highway Central section was an Indian trail—and both won out!

We see now, though, that we should have taken the advice of the friendly Italian priests and gone the usual business travelers' way from Lima to Cuzco—via three days' bus trip to Arequipa and then two days by train. We have decided to fly back to Lima if we can get reservations.

We woke refreshed and rested . . . After a breakfast in the sunshine on the boarding house balcony we were off to arrange our trip to the ruins, buy our airline tickets and see Cuzco in route. The Faucett Peru Aviation Company office had just two reservations left for each. So we could sit back and enjoy Cuzco—the unchanged Spanish houses on narrow cobbled streets, Indians and llamas hurrying by right across the main plaza—heavy carved wooden doors, elaborate old churches—altogether a story book town—the most unchanged Latin American town of any size I ever have seen (40,000 people). Whole blocks of houses are built right on Inca foundations with their elaborate stone masonry—the narrowest little streets, no wider than sidewalks at home—are lanes dating from the days of the Inca city, and the heavy stone foundations along them stand five feet above my head.

Macchu Picchu

After I came back from Macchu Picchu my life seems almost to be divided into "before I went to Macchu Picchu" and "after I came back." It was surely one of the great experiences of my life, and I have seen most of the famous archeological sites in Mexico and Central America.

Here a pre-Inca people chose a high spectacular ridge surrounded by scenic mountains to build an all stone city reached only by precipitous trails from all directions. On terraces on the steep slopes they planted their corn and potatoes, and fitted larger stones in perfect symmetry, above the terraces, into houses and temples. They were conquered by the Incas, in spite of their inaccessibility, and taught the Incas the art of fitting stones. The Inca empire moved most of the people into the more fertile open valleys, but when the Spaniards came, the priests, the Vestal Virgins and some members of the royal family fled here, where they lived undiscovered by the Spaniards till all had died or had mixed in with the peasant Indians of tiny mountain villages ten and twelve kilometers away. No one remembered the existence of the city. A few Indians knew there were great stones piled on the top of the ridge a thousand feet above the river. Such an Indian told Hiram Bingham, the Yale University anthropologist and explorer, in 1912—Yale archeologists took one hundred forty mule loads of objects out of the ruins, cleared the vegetation, and finally got the Peruvian government to build a narrow gauge road along the river to the foot of Macchu Piccho's cliff.

The ruins are indescribable covering about a hundred acres— roofless peaked stone houses, fortified round towers, beautifully smoothed stone temples, an "astronomical observatory" at the top most point up many stair steps—bathing places along a water conduit—dungeon chambers with holes for the hands like the Puritan stocks—and all the hillside down to the steep cliff terraced for elaborate gardens.

We left Macchu Picchu regretfully at noon the second day, making our way by mule back to the river. There the "autocarril" or bus-on-tracks was waiting to take us back up the beautiful river canyon to another ruin at Allantay Tambo. We climbed the hill to the fort and heard the nice guide tell the story of the Inca general Allanta, who asked for the daughter of the Cuzco Inca and who was refused. There was a war, Allanta and the princess were imprisoned, but escaped to build this city Allantay Tambo. From this well-known legend an Argentinian wrote the most famous South American opera.

Though the spirit is willing the flesh is weak

So we have two days to kill in Barranquilla (Columbia) —our last in South America. I toy with the idea of going by bus to the interesting old Spanish city of Cartagena, eighty miles down the coast. But it is three hours on the bus (one of those typical South American buses on an unpaved road)—Morle and Donny do not want to go (Donny has a Barranquilla chum he met on the boat who is taking him around town). I want to see Cartagena's old Spanish fortifications built to ward off English pirates, but though the spirit is willing the flesh is weak. My spirit is tired of long hot lonesome trips on buses. I am weary of looking for new places to stay overnight, talking Spanish to strangers after dark. Besides, it is very hot and the swimming in Barranquilla tempts me to stay.

We discovered a bus that went eleven miles to Barranquilla's ocean beach. (The city itself is up the river mouth.) At the beach, Puerto Colombia, we found a bath house and pavilion where Donny and I could change to bathing suits and Morle could sit on a shaded *veranda and watch the sea. The beach itself was taken up by returned fishermen, their rowboats, their children, their fish cleaning, and their pigs to eat the fish cleanings—but the sea beyond was fine swimming after a long cold mountain summer—small waves, warm green tropical water, a cool breeze from the trade-wind belt, right off the Caribbean. We returned by dark, to stroll around town and to bed.*

. . . we are delighted, on going for one more check to the Pan American office, to find Morle's former student Harvey Stein, now a geologist in a Texaco oil field nearby, waiting to see us. We had written him hurriedly from Bogota, but felt we had little chance to find him. I was glad I had not gone to Cartagena, for the four of us (plus Donny's chum) spent a happy Sunday driving all over the city and its pretty modern suburbs in a horse-drawn taxi.

Harvey, through his company, had access to the swimming pool of the fanciest hotel we have heard about in South America (The Prado US $9 a day). The pool was in a large patio garden, about two acres in all . . . shade, palm trees, miniature waterfall and white-garbed English-speaking waiters serving drinks and ice cream, young American engineers, geologists and business representatives lolling about the Sunday in town. (This is most of what many Americans ever see of Colombia.)

(Heading for the airport) we still have $80.00 in traveler's checks out of the $800 we brought, but will spend more than half of that in Kingston, Miami, New Orleans and on the train (home). We have to show for the $800 however, not only a summer for three people in three South American countries, but 800 feet of movie film, 200 Kodachrome slide shots, 100 black and white Kodak prints, 20 large water colors, a scrapbook, this diary, and a long line for conversation all the coming winter.

Two happy couples in Mexico City, 1951
left to right: Rosita's doctor husband, Rosita, the author,
and Mr. Henry Morle Bailey, the author's husband

Two happy couples in Mexico City 1951

Unknown ruins painted by Helen Miller Bailey

CHAPTER TEN

Monument to a Young Man

Helen utilized what we would call today a situational leadership approach to helping young people achieve a college education. She seemed to understand and provide just what was needed at just the right moment, regardless of how small or large a commitment on her part. In addition to the temporary homes she provided for a couple dozen, she designed campus jobs, handed out $5 bills in class for gas money, encouraged all to improve performance, and invited all of her students to her home each semester. From conversations with several of Helen's students, the concept of "Doc's magic" emerged. How did she know just exactly what a student needed to make it through that class or that semester? How did she know that her kindnesses would be paid forward with lives dedicated to public service? Intuition? A sixth sense? I think Helen would have liked her story to be told with a nod to the genre of magical realism, a literary gift from her beloved Latin America.

Long before a Chicano movement or ethnic studies courses, Doc Bailey fostered self-efficacy and self-respect through her confidence in students' abilities and a deep regard for their ancestry. For literally thousands, she was a positive force in an otherwise unsupportive social, economic, and educational structure.

The more tangible of Helen's great gifts to California's citizenry are the hundreds of students who received, and those who have yet to earn, scholarships from the Helen Miller Bailey Scholarship Fund and its predecessor, the Armando Castro Memorial Scholarship Fund, since 1955.

No record exists of a politician, philanthropist, college professor, or noted physician named Armando Castro in Los Angeles in the 1950s. However, sports section article after article in the *Los Angeles Times* proclaimed the track and field prowess of a Roosevelt High School student by that name in 1953 and 1954. Was it a coincidence that Mr. Bailey had taught science at Roosevelt up until 1955 when polio and a wheelchair ended his teaching career? Was the scholarship fund named after a high school athlete?

And then there it was . . . the nineteen-word announcement on September 18, 1956, in the *Los Angeles Times'* historical archive which read, "'Monument to a Young Man' docudrama airs tonight at 7 p.m. on KABC and recounts the life of Armando Castro."

The youthful receptionist's voice at KABC-TV's news desk chuckled at the call asking about television film footage from 1956. "That's a long time ago," she said incredulously. "I know, but it's important to me," I pleaded. "Can you please check with someone?" Surprisingly, the young woman quickly returned to the line and explained that KABC-TV had donated all historical footage (film aired before 1970) to UCLA's television archives.

The University of California Los Angeles' Powell Library and its Media Arts Instructional Lab are simply magnificent architecturally and technically. Handed a remote control device and told soundproof room 8 was mine for three hours, I sat down, turned on the TV monitor, and the *DuPont Cavalcade Theatre* production began, complete with commercials touting the wonders of chemically treated clothing that needed less ironing and many other technological advances for the midcentury, modern housewife (lured by an adman's iconic promise of "better living through chemicals").

The written-for-TV play related the story of a young Mexican American athlete named Armando Castro who had been stabbed to death trying to break up a fight outside a 1954 New Year's Eve party in East Los Angeles. Some of his fans at Roosevelt High School and classmates at East Los Angeles College (where he had transferred) were depicted in the film asking, "What do you think, Dr. Bailey?"

Yes, the students were gathered in Helen Miller Bailey's office—the connection was established. The young people proudly displayed the princely sum of $8, which they had collected in Armando's memory. They wanted Doc's opinion on whether they should send flowers to the funeral home or plant a tree on campus in Armando's name. Yes, either of those things could be done in 1955 for under $10. Indeed with $8, a person could purchase a week's worth of groceries, or thirty-two gallons of gasoline, forty packs of cigarettes, a four-night stay in a hotel, or twenty-seven haircuts.

Helen had a way of always broadening students' ambitions; she always had a much greater vision for what could be accomplished. So, not surprisingly, she encouraged Armando's friends to set a new goal of $50, which could be used to fund a college scholarship in

Armando's name for a deserving Hispanic high school senior in the San Gabriel Valley area. That day, Helen became the treasurer of a scholarship fund that would provide hope and encouragement to deserving students for decades.

The docudrama's next scene showed Helen; Roosevelt High teachers Evan Thomas, Dave Haskell, and Albert Padilla; Roosevelt High School Counselor George Wooley; and Los Angeles Country Sheriff Deputy Julio Gonzales all meeting in Los Angeles City Councilman Edward Roybal's office. As was Helen's way, the goal of a single $50 scholarship was going to be surpassed. The newly appointed trustees of the Armando Castro Memorial Scholarship Fund were planning a dance as a fundraiser for one of the first scholarship funds established to benefit Mexican American college-bound students.

The $1.50 admission tickets to the dance were so sought-after the event had to be moved to the biggest hall in Los Angeles—the Shrine Convention Ballroom. The $6,000 profit from the first dance funded over thirty college scholarships for students from high schools in the area. The popular Manny Lopez Orchestra performed for free at the first and subsequent dances, "My wife had gone to Roosevelt and like so many others we wanted to support deserving kids from our area," recalled Lopez.

If she danced that night is unknown, but the archived docudrama definitely showed Helen at the dance introducing a promising young man (who was explaining why he wouldn't be attending college next semester), to a beautiful, high-achieving ELAC co-ed—situational leadership? Or as her former students would suggest, just a sprinkling of Doc's magic.

The scholarships had quickly rolled out. On September 20, 1955, at the Council of Mexican American Affairs' meeting at the Statler

Hotel in Los Angeles, Armando Castro Memorial scholarships were also awarded to college students by Los Angeles Police Department Information Division officers Julio Gonzales, Arthur Ruiz and Evan Thomas to Florentino Garza ($300), UCLA law student; Frank Salcedo ($225), UCLA pre-med student; and Peter Sanchez ($225), education major at UCLA.

Annual mention of these fundraising dances is found in the *Los Angeles Times* for several years. The second dance was held on May 26, 1956, at the Shrine Ballroom. On April 7, 1957, the *Los Angeles Times'* announcement of the third dance (April 20, 1957) reported that fifty-six students had already received college scholarship monies from the fund. The sixth annual benefit dance was held on June 18, 1960, at the iconic Hollywood Palladium.

In 1958 Helen Aguilar, an Anaheim Business College student, was the first Orange County resident selected for a scholarship from the fund. In 1960 a second female student, Martha Lydia Casas, received funds to ease her transition from Rosemead High School to East Los Angeles College.

In January two years later, in the office of ELAC President Benjamin Swartz, California State Controller Alan Cranston made a public donation to the Armando Castro Scholarship Fund. "Dropouts, young men and women who discontinue their education, are a particular loss to our national intellectual potential," said Cranston. "In order to keep what President Kennedy calls our brain power at a high level it is necessary that responsible citizens in all segments of our society take immediate steps to help solve this problem. I believe that a partial solution lies in scholarships to needy students."

Cranston explained that in the East Los Angeles area many hundreds of students of Mexican ancestry miss the benefit of college because of lack of funds. "I therefore have decided to make a public contribution . . . to discourage local youngsters from dropping out of school. The work of this organization is very familiar to me and I have seen many people who were given an initial boost by this group who became teachers, engineers, doctors, and prominent members of other professions," he added. "I commend the students of East Los Angeles College, who established the foundation to commemorate the death of one of their colleagues, and compliment Councilman Roybal and Dr. Bailey for their untiring dedication for the success of this worthy program."

Just how many dances were held and what other important donations to the fund were received are not known. However, several of Helen's contemporaries report that at some point she began to fund the Armando Castro Scholarship Fund with proceeds from the sale of her paintings and from her textbook royalty checks.

Numerous Los Angeles area newspaper accounts of her retirement reported that Helen painted some nine hundred works, documenting her world travels. She also painted all of the California missions three times, over several years. Helen is listed as a member of the Los Angeles Art League in 1941. Most of her work sold for $50 per canvas; many were given as gifts to friends and favorite students. Along with other members of The Women Painters of the West, Helen's work was often exhibited at the Wilshire Ebell and other Los Angeles venues.

In the 1992 *Smithsonian* interview Vincent Price (Yale art history degreed collector and famous actor) described the Los Angeles art scene in the thirties and forties as fairly bleak, "...but as I look back on it, there were hundreds of little groups of people fighting desperately to become...a community of artists. There was a group called The Women Painters of the West. Oh, they were wonderful... As a sort of smart-ass actor being interviewed for a fan magazine, I said that it was a shame that The Women Painters of the West were all women because the men were still the best artists...They challenged me to a duel. I never had a better time in my life, and I came to admire these women enormously. The debate was in a packed theater – with me and these ladies. It was great fun."

Upon Helen's retirement in May 1974, colleagues created a scholarship in Helen's name. Her student and close friend Richard Avila explains that much of these "contributions" actually represented purchases of many of Helen's paintings which had been displayed in her office and classrooms while she was still teaching. In July 1974, the account totaled $10,500. (Some years earlier, remaining funds from the Armando Castro Fund had been turned over to Roosevelt High School.)

When Helen passed away in 1976, in accordance with her will, her scholarship fund was increased to total $20,000, in order to create a permanent endowment, which is administered today by ELAC's Foundation. The social sciences faculty selects the recipients each year. (For context, in the early seventies one could easily purchase a three-bedroom, two-bath house in Southern California for $20,000.)

Helen's hand-painted thank-you card sent in July 1974 to each scholarship fund contributor featured a photograph of one of her paintings of Hawaii titled *Skies over Oahu, Hawaii.*

With my heart lifted to the skies, I am thanking everyone involved in the fund raising in honor of my retirement. As of now, the total in the Bailey Scholarship Fund has reached $10,500! It is already invested and two $400 scholarships will be given from the interest in 1975. May your own expectations also soar in this coming year!

The transformative impact of scholarships funded by Helen Miller Bailey can best be described by the recipients. (For letters to Doc Bailey see Appendix B.)

Daniel Garcia
Federal Regulatory Commission, Washington DC

"Is this Professor Soza?" the caller began, "My name is Daniel Garcia. We should talk." A bit concerned, I responded, "I see you are calling from Washington DC. What is this about?" "Helen Miller Bailey saved my life," he replied. "Oh, yes, let's talk."

Garcia explained he was "one of those troubled kids" Helen drew close to her, "many like me can say, if it wasn't for Doc Bailey, I would have been long dead or in jail by now." Instead, nearing the end of his forty-six years of service in various federal government agencies, Garcia shared that he often recollects the personal "crucial conversations" on horseback near the Bailey mountain cabin between 1964 and 1966 when "Dr. Bailey introduced me to my future."

Daniel Garcia survived early childhood living with several families as a result of the early divorce of his parents and his unwitting participation in the Los Angeles County social services system. He often uses the "rags to riches" analogy to describe his life:

> *Mom lived in a small house in back of a Baptist Church above Main Street in downtown Los Angeles and Dad lived on Brooklyn Avenue. The area was called "El Hoyo" or "The Pit." Dad's place was a two-room apartment behind Beto's café.*
>
> *I was shuttled between the two for years until truancy and a fleet-footed police officer's persistence resulted in*

me living with a foster family for a couple of years. The Donovans, my foster parents, lived in Lincoln Heights, which my child's mind fantasized as my "forest." I hid amongst the trees to get away from school and life's difficulties. But the LAPD often found me and took me home to the Donovans.

Beto's was a popular café and bar, owned by my godparents. The weekend scene included rowdy musicians and the cops—showing up both as customers and to stop fights. I called that place "home" too. That's where I learned to cook up tripe for the big pot of menudo. I helped my Madrina wash dishes and take orders. My dad helped my Padrino work the bar. They both carried guns on their belt when working —you had to—it was that kind of place.

During my teen years, home was with my godparents— my Madrina (Nina) Hortencia Shrewsbury and my Padrino (Nino) Albert "Beto" Shrewsbury—in the Monterey Park hills overlooking East Los Angeles College, where my new life was to begin. Living with my Nina and Nino and their children Connie and Albert is how I came to meet Art Torres, my best friend and neighbor.

Art and I went to Bella Vista Elementary School, Eastmont Junior High and Montebello High School together. Although I didn't do well in high school, in 1964, Art convinced me to sign up for a political science class with him at ELAC. Art loved student politics. I loved girls.

My academic salvation was my second love— writing. My answers to Dr. Bailey's essay questions caught her attention and at some point, she reached out to me and for the next two years I enjoyed a grand relationship with her and her husband; I spent many, many weekends at their rustic home at the base of the mountains above Los Angeles. I usually slept in that spare room they had. One of their adopted sons Young Kim was living there at the time. I think he was going to Cal Tech.

I took to riding her horses; I rode into a "real" forest with Doc Bailey, crossing over streams, and soaking up that grand feeling of being out of East LA. I loved our talks on those rides. She always took the lead and I had to keep pace with her not just to be able to hear her questioning and to respond with gusto, but also because honestly I was fearful of getting lost. I always felt like I was in some kind of dream vacation during those weekends. She knew I loved her paintings of the forest, depicting a hide-away in the beauty of nature. Years later she gave me two of these paintings.

As my grades improved I began to consider life after ELAC. That's when Doc Bailey started to teach me the power of giving by having me assist my close friend Art Torres.

Art Torres went on to University of California and has created his own legacy within California and Democratic Party politics.

Dr. Bailey "encouraged" me to attend the eight-week 1966 Summer Encampment for Citizenship at the University of Maryland. Who else but Doc Bailey would have considered me a candidate for such a program and much less foot the expense of my registration. She did, and my Nina and Nino drove me to Washington D.C. The entire summer was spent being exposed to public policy officials and the Washington D.C. environment with close encounter sessions with Senator Robert Kennedy, Stokley Carmichael, and others. That summer and Doc Bailey's continued love and support did two things: pushed me to get into public service and taught me the value of an education. I went on to University of Southern California (USC).

While at USC, Jesus Melendez, an attorney with the Los Angeles School District, Raoul Isais, and I, organized a MASA chapter. To increase membership in the Mexican American Student Association, I combed records in the Registrar's office for any Spanish-surnamed student and called them to join with us. About eight or so accepted the invitation. Jesus and I would also befriend David Sanchez of the Brown Berets and would meet up with him occasionally during those years. Never forgetting my roots, I often took friends from USC to Beto's Café for some great food. I personally poured the menudo. My USC brothers enjoyed some wide-eyed, late night experiences in El Hoyo.

Upon graduation I was hired to educate the Hispanic community of East Los Angeles about government employment opportunities. I also worked in the Watts and Willowbrook areas to attract returning Vietnam veterans to government work. I was involved in setting up the examining standards and qualified applicant screenings for air traffic controllers, postmasters, and cryptographic equipment operators. In 1970 I was one of the first Hispanics selected for the Department of Health, Education and Welfare's (now Health and Human

Services) three-year management intern program. As part of that program, I served the honorable Chet Holifield, who represented the whole of the Eastside of Los Angeles in Congress. So I found myself back in Washington, D.C. Currently, I'm involved with real estate and facilities work here at the Federal Energy Regulatory Commission. I can't say I've been bored!

Daniel Garcia's story provides reinforcement for the power of actions that instill confidence, in this case that small tutoring "job" is an example of one of the ingenious, albeit momentarily seemingly insignificant, devices Helen employed with hundreds of others. Art and Daniel had no idea she was helping position them both to achieve fulfilling careers and lives that matter.

These small acts are the tools many of her students describe as somehow identifying and nurturing potential in them that they never knew existed. Helen was quoted in a June 2, 1974, *Los Angeles Times'* salute, "We're talking about survival here. You've got to keep people going when they're caught with car repairs, bail bonds, traffic fines. This is a matter of helping kids to keep going."

Art Torres
California State Assemblyman and Senator
Vice Chair California Institute for Regenerative Medicine

No one can deny that Art Torres "kept going." He earned his undergrad degree from University of California, Santa Cruz, and his law degree from University of California, Davis. As Garcia mentioned, his friend always loved political life and few have accomplished more for Californians than California State Assemblyman and Senator Art

Torres. His twenty years in the legislature focused on constituent health issues, human rights, and the environment.

He authored numerous clean water bills including the landmark California Safe Drinking Water Act. Chapter 14 describes his impact on ending one of the most egregious healthcare crimes against women in California in the twentieth century. Art Torres co-authored legislation to create both the Japanese American Museum and the Museum of Tolerance in Los Angeles.

Torres's recollections of Helen center on her appreciation of Mexican culture and respect for her students, "Doc Bailey had a way of making you believe in yourself and in your future. We all owe her so much." His admiration for her was evidenced by his attendance at Helen's retirement ceremony and his service as the master of ceremonies at the posthumous dedication of the Helen Miller Bailey Library on the East Los Angeles College campus in 1980, as well as his kind support of this project.

After a successful thirteen years as chairman of the Democratic Party in California, Torres returned to health care issues in his role as vice chairman of the governing board of the California Institute for Regenerative Medicine. He serves as a patient advocate, consistent with all his years of public service.

Félix Gutiérrez, PhD
Professor Emeritus University of Southern California Annenberg School of Communication and Journalism

> *I only had two brief encounters with Helen Miller Bailey, but these were important in the formation of my self-concept and self-confidence.*

We lived in East Los Angeles for most of my life - Belvedere and then Lincoln Heights. My parents were both school teachers in East Los Angeles. My dad succumbed to cancer when I was twelve. After he passed, Mom moved us to South Pasadena because of the good reputation of the schools and community.

So as a teenager I made the move to a very Anglo area. South Pasadena was only five miles from East Los Angeles but about 500 miles in demographic terms. I graduated from South Pasadena High School in 1967.

My mother was active in East Los Angeles in 1967 when I was a high school senior. She went to a meeting one night and ran into Alberto C. Diaz, the editor of the Belvedere Citizen newspaper. He had worked with my dad in the thirties and forties on a newspaper called the Mexican Voice. Diaz asked about the family and Mom mentioned my upcoming graduation. He told her about the Armando Castro scholarships which were the only scholarships I had ever heard of for Mexican Americans. Recipients needed to be the outstanding Mexican-American graduate of their high school, which made for a lot of competition for students at Garfield, Roosevelt, or Lincoln. But that year at South Pasadena High only three other seniors qualified.

I filled out the application and my counselor provided the required recommendation. I mailed the package but received no response until the day of my graduation when a letter arrived announcing my award. I was all proud! Soon a letter from Helen Miller Bailey arrived explaining how to collect my scholarship once I had enrolled in college.

That letter was my first contact with her. The arrangement was that you got $50 if you were going to junior college and $75 if you were going to Cal State. These seem like such small amounts but remember that public college tuition was free in California for two decades based on the state's 1960 Master Plan for Education.

That summer I worked as a gardener for the Los Angeles City Schools; At the end of the summer I was assigned to East Los Angeles College. It was tough work—you got dirty. I noticed a sign on the side of bungalow "Helen Miller Bailey." I walked over with a rake or shovel in my hand.

I knocked on Dr. Bailey's door and asked to come in. Dressed like a gardener, I introduced myself and it didn't register with her right away. I mentioned the scholarship and she said, "oh, umm." Eventually after a little small talk, I said, "I came by to get my money." She responded, "Well I can make out your scholarship check right now," and pulled out the checkbook. "Let's see that will be $50." I corrected her, "Well I'm going to Cal State," which in those days, for a Chicano kid was like saying you were going to Harvard. People did, but it wasn't expected; it wasn't normal.

This I remember very clearly, she looked right at me—I'm sure influenced by my dirty clothes and gardener tools—she said, "You're going to L.A. State?" "Yes." "Well, you go to L.A. State and when you're registered, and when they give you your registration card, then you come back and I'll give you your check for $75."

That $75 was a great reinforcement. It was a reminder that there were people who respected you. In other words, assimilation isn't something you have to do for people to invest in you. For me it was beyond the scholarship. On my way now, I earned my bachelor's degree from Cal State Los Angeles, my master's from Northwestern University, and my doctoral degree from Stanford.

There was a group of students on the Cal State LA campus who had gone to East Los Angeles College and were involved in activities around the Armando Castro Scholarship Fund and its recipients. They sent around occasional flyers. I would hang them on my wall where I studied as a reminder that there were Chicano kids going to college and maintaining their identity.

Part of the Helen Miller Bailey story, as I understand it, is one of the formation and identity of the college. I remember as an elementary school kid, they would take us to ELAC. They built these magnificent structures for the public—the stadium and auditorium first, a lot of the schoolrooms were still in bungalows. They wanted a place for the community. My dad used to take us (he taught at Kern Jr. High in the early fifties) and they would have the music department at Kern book the auditorium and the choir and the orchestra would play. It was a way to get people on the campus. They would have daytime programs when they would bus us from Happy Valley (between Lincoln Heights and El Sereno) and they would take us to ELAC for musical programs and dance performances.

I heard a great story from someone, and I can't attribute this to fact, that Helen Miller Bailey was so proud of the campus when it moved to its own home, on Brooklyn Avenue, that in the early morning hours she used to walk around the parking lot and pick up litter and cigarette butts. She'd walk through the parking lot to make sure it stayed clean. So this very personal commitment was a direct response to strong public agitation around building the school on the Eastside.

Finding an Anglo in those days with the degree of authenticity Helen displayed in her commitment and respect for Chicanos was very unique. Oh, sure there were many who loved Mexican food, our fiestas, and our tequila, but authenticity is not a one-way street. These were the culturally deprived she chose to serve and support without requiring assimilation in return.

Dr. Gutiérrez' is author or co-author of five books and more than fifty scholarly articles on racial or technological diversity in media. He was honored in 2014 by the Los Angeles County Board of Supervisors for his 40 years of exemplary scholarship in journalism and college teaching, having held tenured faculty positions at California State University Northridge, as well as administrative posts with University of Southern California, Stanford University, and California State University Los Angeles.

Helen Miller Bailey reading in her La Cañada home

Amboseli Game Reserve, Tanzania,

Helen Miller Bailey 1963

CHAPTER ELEVEN

The Postcolonial Promise of Rural

Education: 1962 Journal Excerpts Africa

So the summer of 1962 found us set on going all the way round Africa to visit the newly created nations now in the UN, to see what hopes and plans they have for educating their masses, to see the great geographic contrasts and spectacles of falls and rivers, veldts, and jungles, to catch glimpses of as many wild animals as we can in the game preserves. I am more interested in the emerging new nations, Morle in the geography, geology and wild life. To see all we want to will be a very expensive task, but Africa is the last continent save Australia we have not visited, and so this is probably our last summer-long trip in the high-expense bracket. We are getting older and slower, both of us, and trips "on the bum" are harder than they used to be, and very difficult in Africa anyway. We are to go to Ghana, Nigeria, French Congo, Congo Republic, Kenya, Ethiopia, Tanganyika, and the Union of South Africa. We'll end up in Durban on South Africa's east coast, and catch a British steamer going back north along the coast and into Europe via the Suez Canal (a leisurely three weeks on shipboard).

Lest This Seem Sheer Idleness and Waste

So we go to the Travel Center, 461 Boylston Street, L.A., where independent travel for teachers is a specialty. Working with Sabena, the Belgian Airlines which used to specialize in African travel before the Congo debacle, the Travel Center takes my list of things we must see and works up a fabulous itinerary. We are to fly to Brussels the day school is out, then take off for Casablanca in Morocco, Sunday, June 17. After four days' rest in that resort town, we go on down into "Black Africa south of the Sahara." Lest this seem sheer idleness and waste, I have contacted members of the Peace Corps known to students of mine, mission schools where African students now on Fulbright in Los Angeles have studied, and three different native school administrators who have visited East Los Angeles Junior College while studying short courses on school administration at the expense of the State Department at University of Southern California. So I have direct invitations to visit schools in four countries.

To fill my evenings, I have undertaken to "ghost write" a book of biographies of US history heroes for an eighth grade reader (for Harcourt Brace) and have brought along notes on 15 such characters which I worked up on a Dictaphone off and on during the spring. I have 17 rolls of 16 mm movie film and 20 rolls of Kodachrome stills, as well as 16 sheets of water color paper and a set of tubes of tempera casein water colors. Hard to pack all this (plus medical supplies and prescriptions we are both taking) into the 88 pounds of luggage we are allowed. We may have to buy new outfits of warmer clothes when we get far south of the Equator.

Centuries of Time Away

But if I had hoped to relax on the warm beach at Casablanca before setting out for the real Africa, I had not studied the climate. The beach is very choppy and the surf heavy with strong cool winds that make sun basking unpleasant. At the nice French hotel, however, there was a fine, big swimming pool in the garden, and a few other visitors about. Our pre-paid excursion took us round native and European quarters of the town and into the Portuguese fort built in the time of Prince Henry the Navigator.

We hired the same driver the second day and drove the 100 miles to Rabat, real capital of the recently independent kingdom of Morocco, where King Hassan II lives in a fancy place. Here on the small river mouth the Romans had built their farthest west and south town and fortification. Then the Moors—escaping from Queen Isabella—refortified it, drove out Portuguese traders who had settled there and made it the center of Caliphate (center of Islamic government). It was one of the most interesting Arab towns I had seen (too long a desert drive to go to Marrakesh or Fez on the edge of the Sahara) . . . now just three days after school closed, feeling a world of distance and centuries of time away.

First School Contact

Here in Dakar, Senegal, I had my first school contact, and it was very heartwarming. I have often given small loans to an idealistic Negro student at East Los Angeles [College] named Burnis Lewis, now at Los Angeles State. In 1960, I gave him $50 to help finance him to go on a work project (Operation Cross Roads Africa) organized indirectly by Yale Divinity School who wanted a Negro from the West Coast on their pre-Peace Corps student exchange in Africa. Burnis and thirty American white students had worked two months that summer in Senegal building a one-room rural school out of concrete and a gravel access road to it. They had given a fine example of how American students were willing to do heavy manual labor, which is scorned by many African college students.

Off we go into the semi-desert brush twenty miles on a gravel road. In the open desert, mid-way between three little mud hut villages, stands the proud new schoolhouse, painted bright yellow. We walk right in, talk in French to the young man teacher, tell him we come as friends of the Negro student who helped the white students build the school. Suddenly we are heroes. The 58 students, of all ages, are almost all in the same class as the school has been there only two years. The teacher is 20, has a secondary school education from Dakar, in which he got a primary teaching credential in the 12th year, but he was born in a village only 10 miles away. He has very good, new books in French for the children, but only 30 for 58 students.

We took lots of movies of the children and the school, and then were taken to the nearest village to see the chief. He was a great, powerful gray haired Negro in a long Moslem gown. He blessed Morle and me with a special Moslem blessing and gave us gifts of papaya and mangoes from his little oasis garden. He said they had been asking for a school for 20 years, and then the American students had built it for them. Once built the new Senegalese government had sent the young teacher, and UNESCO had sent books.

Late that afternoon, we turned back to the coast and came out at a large village called Cayar, unchanged in 1,000 years. There the people, all in long Moslem gowns and elaborate, tied-up turbans, were hauling in dug-out canoes and large fishing nets in the sunset light. Figuring ten men to the net and boat crew, and 200 boats, there were 2,000 people working on the beach. I took photos as long as the light lasted, although the women cleaning the fish were insulted and started throwing fish tails at me.

World Without a Bomb Conference

A big Pan American plane en route to Johannesburg from New York took us on to Accra, capital of Ghana. It first set down in Monrovia, Liberia; I had considered this little principality of the Firestone Rubber Company one place that could be passed by. The plane went on under the bend of Africa into an area of a heavy wet season in mid-summer, and we came down at Accra.

Here Kwame N'Krumah, anti-white, anti-British and busy getting both US and Russian economic aid in open competition, has built a republic out of the area the British called the Gold Coast. Actually he is not doing badly. His Ghana pound exchanged equally with British sterling. [N'Krumah ruled Ghana, formerly the Gold Coast, from 1951 to 1966.]

The rainy season has been so heavy that towns in the interior are flooded and the daily Accra newspaper is full of pictures of towns abandoned and school houses caving in, up country. This puts a cramp in my school visiting program. A native principal of the secondary school at Keta, 130 miles from Accra, had been one of the State Department's guests at the USC short course for foreign school administrators. I had been in charge of entertaining him for a day at the Junior College in 1961. He had written me urging me to take a taxi on the road to Keta where he would meet us halfway with the school's car. (Unfortunately) for a week there has been no road, nor telegraph, nor telephone connection with Keta, across the flood. Somehow the principal sent me an air letter telling me to contact Mr. Davis at the USIS library in Accra, who would help me see some schools in the capital at any rate.

When I called the USIS (the United States Information Service) they asked me to come watch them move their students' library to a new building N'Krumah had just offered them a mile from the U.S. Embassy. They had 6,000 books—3,000 Ghana school children were to join in a "school book parade," with a fife and drum corps, carrying two books each. I met several native secondary school teachers, both men and women, who were delighted to have their parade photographed by an American teacher.

Sad thing was the books themselves. For shame on Americans sending such old battered, boring books! Statistical Abstract of 1915. The Citrus Industry in 1920. Not one new colorful book to appeal to children, though each child gleefully took the two given him, along with a balloon marked "USIS Book Parade," and marched the 15 blocks down the main street with a sort of jazzy lilting step.

Every tenth child carried a hand lettered placard on a high pole—"Read! Read! Read!"—"Books are the mark of progress!" "Reading turns savagery to civilization!" "Can you Read? Well, Why not?"—all making a good movie. The children ranged from six years to university students. The new library was not even finished, so the children put the 6,000 books in neat piles on the floor (no Dewey

*Decimal System!) and marched out singing and waving the balloons.
N'Krumah had sent several news photographers and reporters.*

*There was little room in the papers for the story, however.
Suddenly the hotel was filled with delegates to the "Conference on
the World Without a Bomb" called to start a "World Wide Movement
headed by Kwame N'Krumah." The streets were full of decorations
and banners, the hotel full of Chinese students and earnest Hindu
ladies and bearded European professors. N'Krumah gave a banquet
for the 120 delegates and the entire Ghana Parliament. All the Ghana
ladies were in the most elaborate native costumes of yellow silk and
orange turbans, and the men in flowing orange and black striped
robes. N'Krumah was there himself and I stood close to him a second
in the crowded hotel lobby. In spite of the other native costumes, he
had on a tuxedo.*

*The resolutions the delegates made were printed and distributed
all 'round the hotel, and sounded like those the "mock conferences"
of the high school World Friendship Clubs used to pass in my days
at Manual Arts High School in the 1930s. The main resolution was
that the conference would set up a permanent executive committee
to establish the "World Without the Bomb" and N'Krumah would be
its standing chairman. He gave the committee a piece of cleared land
and promised to build them a fine headquarters.*

Timbuctoo Couldn't Have Been Any Better

*Our next stop was to be in Nigeria (more progressive and
democratic than Ghana) where we were to take a side plane trip to
Kano. We had both wanted to go to Timbuctoo but service is only
bi-weekly since the French Sudan became an independent state and
the French guest hotel has been discontinued and we might have*

been stuck two weeks in the desert with no place to stay. I was willing to settle for Kano, about which I had read a recent article by Lowell Thomas. It has for 1,500 years been the head of camel caravans beyond and north of the Niger River across the Sahara, and connected with the Gulf of Guinea by a Niger River tributary.

Compass Travel sent a car and a tall black Moslem guide in a long flowing embroidered robe. He took us out of the European town, across the river and grassland between and into the mud-walled city. He also took us back 1,000 years in history. It couldn't have been any better for photographs. The native market was one of the most interesting I have ever seen. Black Moslem women sit cross-legged on adobe platforms spinning cotton with thumb and distaff. Many craftsmen were weaving and dyeing the bright cotton cloth for the long robes everyone wears, and the indigo head dresses of the Tuaregs who come in off the Sahara to buy them. No one minded being photographed. It seemed like an Arabian Nights market . . .

The same guide led me up to the highest mezzanine on the old adobe mosque, (I had never been allowed to go up to the "mezzanine" of a mosque before, being a Christian and a woman) and I got panoramic photos of the town, the walls, the Emir's adobe palace, and the grasslands leading off to the desert. I forgot all about my longing for Timbuctoo, which is 400 miles up along the Niger. We saw armor, in a room of the Emir's palace open to visitors, which is still worn in horseback fights, which looked like chain mail of the time of the Crusaders. Then dinner, overnight, and back on the London-Rome-Kano-Lagos-Nairobi-Johannesburg jet with its 100 passengers and on to Lagos, Nigeria.

Most Girls Get Married at 15

We spend the next day visiting schools in Lagos. A Nigerian student has attended ELAJC for the last two years and I have been his advisor as a sociology major. He had given me letters to the high school he came from and then had written to the principal that I was coming. All the high schools in Lagos had been founded by missionaries or private groups and now had been taken over by the Nigerian government. But the salaries were better and religion could still be taught if the parents so wish. This school still had the name Boys Methodist High School.

Though almost every Nigerian child gets four years of primary school, only two or three thousand get any secondary education. It is almost all college preparatory, getting ready for the "Cambridge" (of Nigeria) at Ibahdan. Only about one-third of the secondary school graduates ever go on to Ibahdan or either of the two schools in Lagos. The principal was delighted that I came, took me to every classroom, where I was met with cheers as a friend and teacher of a famous alumnus.

I was taken to the Girls Methodist High School, where 200 girls were busy taking entrance examinations. Only 60 of them would be admitted to the freshman class, of which only 20 would ever stay to graduate. Few Nigerians are interested in girls' education, as most leave to get married at 15.

At the other girls' high school in Lagos, one with 120 pupils supported by the Nigerian government and called "The New Era Girls Secondary School," there is a member of the US Peace Corps teaching English composition. She is a Negro girl from Los Angeles State College (Lillian Miles) who knew I was coming and had been trying to reach me. Here a Dr. Proctor, Negro head of a small colored college in West Virginia, heads up a staff of three white Americans, who are in charge of 107 Peace Corps teachers now in Nigeria. Three hundred fifty more are to come in September, and many more are being requested by the Nigerian government. English is the official language and the tribal people have no way of learning it at all.

Two young American men teachers of the Peace Corps came in to see me at Lillian Miles' request, arriving by motor scooter from their school ten or fifteen miles out. They were both the peppy, athletic type, teaching English but organizing sports too, working up nature-study program, helping build new dormitories, and leading glee clubs, all with tireless enthusiasm. Miss Miles took me to the Nigerian National Museum where we saw a fine anthropology collection from the rain-area tribal groups and grasslands people near Kano. There was also an exhibit from the newly discovered archeological sites at Ife in the ancient kingdom of Ghana, that were proving settled towns existed in the Niger Valley in the early Bronze Age (2,000 BC)

An Army of Teachers

The next morning we said goodbye to Nigeria and flew by Pan Am to Leopoldville in the former Belgian Congo. We knew, of course, that the Belgians had left the Congo area, and it had been in a state of governmentless chaos for nearly two years, save for the UN forces. In April a group of African educators visiting USC had come out to ELAJC to spend the day and I had been hostess for a young Mr. Lembo, whom I subsequently asked to dinner. He was in charge of four rural schools near Leopoldville, and he had urged me to see his wife and children there, as well as to contact his own immediate superior, a lady named Gabrielle Bequet, as well as the English teacher in his own old high school, a Miss Clark.

196

Our travel agent had told us to bring international police certificates of good conduct (a form easily obtained from the Los Angeles County Sheriff's Office) and several extra copies of photos, if we got into difficulty in any of the new nations. But the visa service contacted by the LA Travel Center had thought a Congolese visa didn't even exist. (We had arranged visas for all other places.) All our documents did not break the immigration officer's stony glare.

Meanwhile the plane we had come in on left for Johannesburg, and no other plane was scheduled to go anywhere else till noon next day. Because Pan Am did not mention a Congolese visa requirement, I sought out the help of a Pan Am pilot and hostess, who in turn enlisted the help of a French doctor. But with their better (than mine) French they could not budge the immigration office. When they puzzled why we had been crazy enough to come, I talked about contacting Mr. Lembo's friends, the lady school administrators. The doctor beamed with relief. Why, they were the heads of the Salvation Army Mission schools. They were French and Canadian missionaries who had been so well-liked by the Congolese when the Belgian Catholic school administrators were expelled, that they had all been put on the government payroll! (Long story short) we were given a 12 hour pass and went into the city, a long dark scary ride, with a Congolese taxi driver provided by the Pan Am hostess. At the hotel we found out that only one plane goes to Nairobi, Kenya, a week. We have no choice but to stay five days in Leopoldville.

On our second day, Salvation Army Colonel Hausdorp and his wife took us across the Congo [River] to French Equatorial Africa... From 1935 to 1946 these dear people had worked among the French convicts in Devil's Island...and had been able to get the new French Republic in 1946...to abandon the colony altogether. Then they had been assigned to Brazzaville, capital of French Equatorial Africa.

In 1929 I had written a very erudite master's thesis in Berkeley, at the "mature" age of 20, when I thought I knew everything and had seen nothing but Modesto. The subject was, "French Equatorial Africa, the Diplomatic History Connected with Brazzaville."...it traced the debates in the French Parliament over the first colony in 1870, the bickering with Belgium and Germany over boundaries up to 1914. Actually I don't think it ever occurred to me that Brazzaville was a real town, on a real river, with real people living there. So now in 1962, thirty-three years later, I am actually there. The World Health Organization has its headquarters for all Africa (malaria control) in Brazzaville.

Saturday, July 6—The highest ranking Salvation Army officer, an English man born in Canada, with a French wife, "Lieutenant General" Frank Evans and Mrs. Evans, took us on their monthly visit to their "bush" stations, a large dispensary and a teacher-training school for primary teachers at Kosabongu about 20 miles out, in heavily wooded, hilly country. The school was out for the holidays but we met the dedicated Swiss "Salvationist" couple who administer its regular staff of 20 and its 300 students. There is a large rural primary school where the students do a year of practice teaching. Actually they come there as primary graduates themselves, and do the practice teaching at the level we would call high school seniors. But of course there is a great demand for them, and the Congo cannot wait to give its primary teachers four years of college. The Salvation Army now has 400 native primary teachers and 10,000 students under its jurisdiction.

The following day was Sunday and the school principal, Madame Gabrielle Becquet, with the vice principals, two Salvationist "Majors" born in Holland, had asked me to attend native services with them.

Heathen that I am, I could hardly refuse. This church had been founded by Mr. Lembo's grandfather as the first Salvationist convert.

As the distinguished American friend of Mr. Lembo, I was asked to speak, which I did in French until my accent proved to be a problem and I was asked to speak in English, which a tri-lingual Dutch lady put into slow simple French, which one of the neat high school boys put into Lingala, the tribal language of that region of Leopoldville. I said Salvationists in America were very respected because of their help to the poor, sick and homeless old people. I added that Salvationists in Los Angeles had been very good to Mr. Lembo and explained how the Fulbright has given him a four year scholarship, and he would be qualified to be the Minister of Education for the Congo. I assured them that God was watching over him there as He did here. I ended in French by saying, "Je crois que tout le monde est sous la commande du meme Dieu!" (I think all the world is under the care of the same God!" which brought drums, hallelujahs, and hurrahs for five minutes.

Then an old lady rose to say that the Salvation Army had brought respect for all religions to the Congo, and had shown that women could be preachers and teachers as well as men. I had always been rather cynical about missionaries, but after I had seen the clinics and schools these dedicated Salvationists run, and the devotion of the people to them, I have to hold my cynicism.

During the next two days, going out along twice to check our air tickets on to East Africa, I was accosted on the street three times by natives who had heard me at the service and wanted to shake my hand and embrace me again. And all this started because a young Congolese educator is studying at USC and visited East Los Angeles College!

Post War Abyssinia (Ethiopia)

The plane was filled with a Congolese youth group going to a conference at the big native college of Makerere, the finest college in Africa, on Lake Victoria. We crossed the area called Ruanda Urundi, which had been declared an independent nation only two days before. Its airport was deserted due to the celebrations, and no one even checked us as transit passengers. So we just go on the same plane and went on to Nairobi, the big, modern sophisticated English city which is the capital of Kenya. We were overnight there briefly and then on by Ethiopian Airways, a 3-hour flight to Addis Ababa, capital of Ethiopia. Of the 10,000 European people in Haile Selassie's 250,000 population capital, more than half of them (5,000 plus) are Greeks, Armenians, Lebanese, or Turks who are running all the businesses.

The next morning a young Greek took us on a 100 mile drive down through rugged semi-desert country to a small resort on a crater lake. Here was also an interesting native town called Debra Zeit, centered around a very ancient Coptic Christian Church. We had a nice lunch of shish kabob and rice pilaf at a resort for "Caucasian" personnel, and then wandered round the little lake, taking pictures of natives washing clothes and watering herds. The great grandfather of Haile Selassie had imported eucalyptus trees from Australia, and now they are growing everywhere in the high central part of the country forming a basis for the economy—firewood, lumber, thatch, and oil. On the second day we went above to Addis Ababa to Mount Entoto, at 9,500 feet, a hill entirely covered with eucalyptus.

Addis Ababa itself looks quite modern and spacious, stretched out below the mountain and rambling over many smaller hills. Haile Selassie, "our revered emperor" has torn down many pre-war

(WWII) government buildings and built modern ones. Many of these buildings are dedicated to the brave Ethiopians (Abyssinians) who were massacred and executed by the Italians during Mussolini's occupation 1934 to 1943. Haile is considered the direct descendant of the son of the Queen of Sheba and King Solomon, born after her visit to Jerusalem about 900 BC. So his is the oldest unbroken ruling line of Kings on earth. (He lives) in a rather unpretentious palace, part of which he is turning over to classes of the expanding "Haile Selassie University" next door. He is also called the "Lion of Judah," and keeps about 300 desert-type North African lions in cages in the central plaza. They are very closely crowded and look more unhappy than most zoo lions.

The city population (except those in the new modern houses) lives in huts made of eucalyptus lumber and roofed with galvanized iron or eucalyptus leaf thatch. What a desolate country this must have been before the eucalyptus was introduced! Moslems and pagans live side by side with Coptic Christians, though that ancient type of Christianity, introduced into Ethiopia via the Blue Nile in about 350 A.D., is the official court religion.

We did see schools, by the dozen, high schools, a big teacher-training school, a medical school, hospitals and clinics in various parts of the city, all founded by and supported by Haile Selassie, in his attempt to westernize the country before he dies (his favorite son and heir was killed in an auto accident two years ago, the remaining son does not get along with the emperor very well). We received a very favorable impression, and were sorry to leave after three days. We also pleased to hear that 350 Peace Corps teachers are coming to teach English in Haile Selassie's secondary schools this September.

On the plane back, we met two Americans who are stationed with the US Information Service in Addis Ababa, going to Kenya for vacation. We found them very soured on the country, however. The hereditary nobility, the army officers, and the church officials do not consider Ethiopia a "new, developing nation," but a proud, ancient nation, which does not need any "development"—loans, yes, but technical advice, no!

These "aristocrats" think Ethiopia should be the leader in all New African nations as the one and only true African state. The Americans said it was much harder to work with them, in regards to libraries, clinics, nurses' training, etc., than with native leaders in other African nations who have come up from the common people and are eager for technical advance.

Cecil Rhodes's South Africa

Next day the driver took us all round the Cape of Good Hope, which is 45 miles or so below Cape Town, South Africa. There were orchards and vineyards, many seaside suburbs, and two game reserves on the way—a very scenic trip. On the way back I went through the home of Cecil Rhodes, British Empire builder who developed gold and diamonds up in the interior, and saw a picture history of his life there. He had come to Cape Town to die of tuberculosis at nineteen, and lived to be 50 and one of the richest men in the world. Famous for founding the Rhodes scholarships, he was actually a very selfish and ambitious man. He is a hero to South Africans, English-speaking ones that is, and there is a great memorial for him on a small hill below Table Mountain. We also went through one of the most elaborate old houses of the Dutch Colonial landlords who began in 1715 to make a fortune in wines and vineyards.

Cape Town is a beautiful seaside and hillside city with thousands of trees and profusely blooming gardens. Dominated by English businessmen in international trade, it is tolerant towards the Indians, mulattoes and native Africans who make up two-thirds of its population. The two English language papers we read are very anti-Boer (the Dutch speaking farmers who settled here between 1700 and 1800) and all the editorials were opposed to the stiff segregation policy of the present Dutch (or Afrikaans) prime minister. In Johannesburg we also read two English dailies and found the same constant criticism of "apartheid" as the segregation policy is called.

But the two drivers we had in Johannesburg, though of British descent, were very "pro-apartheid," and never missed a chance to call the black Africans "baboons" or "savages," who did not have "sense enough to appreciate the fine slum-clearance housing" the mine owners had provided for them. Of course in Johannesburg there are seven such African working men and miners for every white man in town. When I asked to see the new housing or any places where natives were allowed to live (in either Cape town, Johannesburg, or Durban) I was always told that the driver "would be fired if he showed native locations to American tourists," and that when I went out into the "bush" I could see plenty of "savage natives" living the way "they like to live." I did not want to visit the mines and missed the chance to see the native miners put on inter-tribal dances every Sunday (encouraged by the mine owners to keep the miners "tribal savages"). So we had chosen to go to Kruger Park on a three-day drive down from Johannesburg across the Transvaal.

(Not finding the opportunities for photographing wildlife satisfying in Kruger) we took out for warmer Durban, which seemed like San Diego in our winter. Here again the people gladly posed as the driver ordered. But they were only half-naked women and children as their men are all away on contract, working in the Natal coal mines a year at a time. The round huts were neat and whitewashed, there was *adequate water in the river at the bottom of the valley and the driver said the "people live as well as they have centuries what with the men bringing home two or three hundred dollars in wages at the end of their year's contract (since they get their pay all at once).*

Again I got the impression that the tourists are only allowed to see the poorest natives who learned the least, so that visitors will consider the black Africans as unteachable, inferior peoples. In these ten days in the Union of South Africa (now called the Republic of South Africa) I got no chance to talk to any native, meet any teachers or students in any way, but could only judge from the English language papers as to the seething tension between Dutch Boers and British, between white and black, with the thousands of Hindus and mixed peoples in Durban and Cape Town caught in between.

After spending my whole quota of "curio" money (tanned zebra skin, native wood carvings) we are here on the S.S. Kenya Castle (a glorified freighter) from August 16 to September 13, spending every night aboard (our fifth crossing of the Equator).

I took the last of my African movies near Mombasa, at Freedtown, a happy-go-lucky village of native fishing people, descended from all kinds and tribes of people who were freed from the Arab slavers by the English in the 1870s. (The Portuguese had lost power and left a century before.)

The rest of the people on the ship were all British. They were either colonial civil servants going home—some for good, some on leave to return to the new nations as agricultural or health experts or else disgruntled business men angry at the new Negro leaders in Kenya and Tanganyika. Those from Rhodesia and Durban were very smug in their "secure" position against any native control. Actually they were all reserved and not over-friendly to Americans. There were three Moslem Indian families going to London on business, but not an African face to be seen anywhere, in the crew, among the stewards or the passengers. No one really talked about Africa or seemed to care about it at all.

It took us a day to creep slowly through the sandy ditch which is the Suez Canal. We were in a convoy of 14 freighters and oil tankers. So into the Port Said we go in the middle of the night, and out the next morning early into the Mediterranean.

If I had not kept up this journal, pasted a big scrapbook full of maps, travel circulars and post cards of the whole trip, and finished up my fourteen large water-colors, I would have forgotten we had been in Africa. Strange to come for three weeks on such a British boat, and then land at Naples and fly home from Rome. But when my zebra skin and native curios arrive home by mail, and I get movies and stills developed, I can surely prove we have been all 'round Africa. Actually we had visited fourteen different countries or provinces, and had traveled more than 25,000 miles, the distance 'round the earth at the Equator. It had cost us less than fifteen cents apiece per mile all told. (Not counting the $30 for the zebra skin!)

See digitized film shot by Helen during this African trip at University of Southern California's Hefner Moving Images Archive Website - http://uschefnerarchive.com/project/baileyfilms/ .

Helen and Morle with zebra skin in late 1960s

Mountains above Cape Town,
South Africa, Helen Miller Bailey

CHAPTER TWELVE
Light My Fire: A Student's Memoir

At the end of a final class meeting of Western Civilization 101 in the spring of 1970, having covered the scheduled lesson plan, Doc Bailey launched into a most curious tirade, "We're nearing semester's end. My guess is many of you have sweethearts and might consider this a fine time to marry!"

Her usual welcoming smile was gone. She seemed angry—all fired-up—where was she going with this? Marriage wasn't exactly a topic addressed in this history class. Yet, there she was, this petite figure in traditional Mexican *blusa* and flowing skirt, owning all the territory in front of the chalkboard with a glare fiercely shifting from one of my male classmates to another. It wasn't too difficult to pick them out since 90 percent of the class of fifty, or so, consisted of young men qualifying for a draft deferment. No Vietnam for them, at least while they stayed in school. East Los Angeles College was then somewhat of a paradise for young, single, and not-too-serious female students.

Doc continued, her voice gaining altitude and conviction, "on that account, DO NOT let me ever hear that any one of you ever purchases a diamond ring!"

Okay, now she had the attention of all eight young women in the classroom too. Was she mad? Of course we would soon be looking for a diamond—the biggest one our boyfriends could afford. Doc didn't let up.

> *Trust me on this, diamonds are not rare. They wouldn't have much value at all if the company that controls all the mines were to stop hoarding the stones to artificially inflate prices. I wish you could have been with me in South Africa in 1962. Though I chose not to visit the disgraceful conditions of the gold and diamond mines, which I have read so much about, I witnessed the near slavery plight of the workers and their families in the towns outside the mines. These inhumanities are all perpetrated on some of the poorest people on Earth so that you can comply with some ad man's prescription for a lonely heart. The jewelry store sales people will even provide you with a formula for spending some ordered multiple of your wages so you can demonstrate the depth of your love in gold and diamonds.*
>
> *If you desire to become a more educated person and to understand the hardships of our brothers in Africa, please read Cry, the Beloved Country by Alan Paton for your book report in Western Civilization II next semester.*

The author describes deplorable gold mining conditions and the degradation of rural South African society in the 1940s. Today's gold and diamond mines are operated with similar disregard for dignity, fairness, or worker safety.

No teacher before or since has ever shown so much heart to me. Oh, I had those who cuddled me as a little girl, others who praised me and told my parents how much they loved having me in their class. This was different. Helen was on fire and the blaze was spreading. Several of us checked the book out of the library during the next semester; many cried through much of the heart-breaking epic. I reported on the book at a gathering of over one hundred students at the Baileys' mountain home—I was on fire.

A few days after delivering my book report, Helen asked me to stay after class; she wanted to know if I could use some extra money (she knew I'd been working at a dry cleaners since I was 15). Most students said, "Yes," to Doc Bailey because she was charming, worldly, the most highly educated woman we knew, while conveying a kind of grandmotherly caring. I nodded in agreement and she explained a project to create study guides for blind students who wanted to take history classes.

Doc said she would provide me with chapter questions related to our text. (This was well before publishers began providing test banks along with instructor editions.) After she checked my answers, I would record both questions and answers on a device in the library and sight-impaired students could listen to the tapes with headsets.

I was confused. Shouldn't she have assigned a project like this to an "A" student? After all, I was much too involved in the "paradise" conditions described earlier to worry about being a worthy student. Somewhat in disbelief, I accepted the job offer and collected my first paychecks from a college. Today I wonder if she considered raising my self-image as part of her responsibility as a teacher. Or as she did with so many, did she simply spot a flicker of potential and think it would be interesting to pour a little lighter fluid on it? When I was hired as a community college tenure track instructor at age fifty-five, the thought occurred to me that Helen had put me on this path so long ago.

I often wonder about the people who never have a Doc Bailey in their lives. I can't help but believe some of those we label "less fortunate"—homeless, drug addicts, prostitutes, and criminals— might have been able to rise from humble beginnings, escape poverty, addiction, and crime, if a Doc Bailey had appeared at just the right time in their lives.

When I married in 1971, shortly after leaving East Los Angeles College, my engagement ring did include the biggest diamond my young husband could afford. That marriage lasted just five years. By the time I remarried in 1983, wiser influences guided my behavior; I did not choose a diamond ring, rather, I opted for a true gem as a lifelong partner. Over thirty years later, no diamonds are found in our home.

In 2005, when I had decided to research Helen's life, a copy of Paton's 1955 novel, along with copies of the several college textbooks Helen authored, found their way into my "shopping cart." These books became the foundation for my endeavor—concrete connections to this woman who was being revealed at first simply by conjuring up my own memories. I was soon to learn that Helen's humanity had indeed been a wildfire engulfing several miles around our college on Los Angeles' Eastside. I was also soon to realize my purpose was greater than to recount her life's works, but to re-ignite the lingering sparks of her legacy.

By 2002, like several Bailey students, I had come around to teaching. Somehow success in the corporate world was not going to be enough to mark my time on Earth. So many of us caught in the maelstrom of one of her passionate lectures, chuckle when we explain Doc's guiding hand at work in our decision to seek teaching positions right out of college or later in life. Former California Deputy Attorney General Richard Avila mused, "Helen always wanted me to be a teacher, not a lawyer, I've been teaching history now for ten years—I guess she finally got her way."

In that interview with Helen's former student and close friend, I recounted my small story to explain my brief relationship with Dr. Bailey. When I got to the part where I questioned why she had chosen me for the assignment, without hesitation, Richard explained, "That's just what she did. That was one of Helen's many gifts. She identified the givers and nurtured them in one way or another so they would have the opportunities and careers which would position them to make the greatest impact on society."

Okay, I finally understood. I was officially part of the club, the givers. I had admired each one I met and interviewed, and wondered why I instantly felt so close to them; they were, really strangers after all, except, we had all experienced Doc's magic.

I teach community college students who are considering a career in business. I've never found a better case for the power of marketing than that perpetrated by the diamond industry; i.e., the DeBeers Company. In addition to the many academic articles published on the subject, the film industry has produced two versions of Alan Paton's novel and the more contemporary *Blood Diamond*. In addition to these materials, I share a story Helen told us as part of that 1970 (supplemental) lecture. The plot remains quite intriguing, although, as yet uncorroborated. Related to DeBeers' complete control of the diamond industry for nearly one hundred years, Doc presented a twisted, and situationally positive, aspect of the monopoly.

For context, it must be explained that weapons of war require access to industrial grade diamonds for drilling, grinding, and polishing precision instrumentation. Today these hardest of gems are becoming equally requisite in high tech electronic equipment since diamonds are the very best heat insulator, which all electronic devices need. The faster the microprocessor, the more heat is generated, the more cooling is required. In March 2011 researchers at the Georgia Tech Research Institute reported development of a solid composite material, made of silver and diamond to cool small, powerful microelectronics used in defense systems. Diamonds provide the bulk of thermal conductivity, while the silver suspends the diamond particles within the composite.

In her 1970 lecture Dr. Bailey explained that for fifty years before and throughout the years since WWII the Belgium-based DeBeers cartel had controlled 80 percent of the global diamond supply from their mines in South Africa. (The diamond mines of India had long since been depleted after one hundred years of excavation.) At the time of the Great War only one other place on earth was known to have diamonds in plentiful supply—Arkansas, USA—indeed, the stones can still be found lying on the ground after a spring rain washes away another slice of topsoil, although no professional mining company has sustained operations there.

Doc claimed that in the years leading up to WWII, the United States government convinced DeBeers' owners, Ernest Oppenheimer and his financier J. P. Morgan, not to supply the Nazis with industrial grade diamonds, in exchange for our promise never to allow development of a commercial diamond mine in Arkansas. That arrangement, she suggested, was a little-known, but a no less important contribution to the Allies' WWII victory. Thereby, DeBeers remained in total control of the supply of diamonds for decades until diamonds were discovered in Russia, Botswana, Angola, Namibia, Australia, Democratic Republic of Congo, and Canada.

The Public Broadcasting television program *Frontline* aired "Diamond Empire" in 1994. Interviewed on that episode, historian John Henderson stated that according to Justice Department records, Samuel W. Rayburn, former president of Bankers Trust of Little Rock and other principals of the Arkansas Diamond Corporation met in the office of JP Morgan with Oppenheimer in attendance. Exactly what transpired is unknown, but the mine superintendent was telegraphed to shut the mine down and prepare for sustained closure.

The made-for-television report included an interview with Professor of Economics Walter Adams, of Michigan State University, who further claimed that as WWII approached, the United States wanted to stockpile industrial diamonds to manufacture armaments for the Allied nations. Worried that London, where 80 percent of DeBeers' stock was warehoused, could fall to the Nazis, our government sought to get the diamonds out of harm's way as there was no other immediately available cache of the already-mined stones in the world. But DeBeers feared the Americans might flood the market with diamonds after the war, which would erode prices; they balked at the idea. Eventually, through a series of complicated talks, the United States did get the diamonds needed through shipments from London to Canada.

If Hitler didn't have access to industrial diamonds, how did he arm Germany? Also reported in the *Frontline* feature, investigators found that diamonds were smuggled in large numbers from the Belgian-owned mines in Africa in packages labeled "Belgian Red

Cross." Delivered to Switzerland, the boxes were forwarded on to Belgium, which was occupied by the German military.

On July 9, 2004, *New York Times'* Steven Labaton reported that DeBeers pleaded guilty to a ten-year-old price fixing charge, which had prohibited the direct sales of their stones into the US market (the largest consumers of the gems). Labaton added, "The company, founded by Cecil Rhodes and other investors in 1880, came under criticism from United States officials during World War II for refusing to provide industrial diamonds for the [Allies'] war effort . . ."

Although we have these conflicting reports, what is not in question is that today anyone who wants to bring a sand pail and trowel to Diamond Crater State Park in Murfreesboro, Arkansas, can, for an entrance fee of $7, dig around and keep any diamonds (or other gems) they find. "Finders Keepers" is the park's motto. Indeed, one of the rarest diamonds in the world, the Strawn-Wagner diamond (the most perfect gem the American Gem Society has ever certified), was found at the park in 1900. Hillary Clinton was loaned the 4.25 carat Kahn Canary diamond, found by a logger at the park in 1977, to wear at her husband's 1993 and 1997 presidential inaugural galas. The largest stone reported to have been found at the park is the 40.23 carat Uncle Sam diamond, uncovered in 1924.

While teaching history Dr. Helen Miller Bailey went to great lengths to reveal the contemporary and larger world to her underprivileged and somewhat cloistered students. Many good teachers find a way to incorporate relevant and powerful imagery into a lecture. Helen, on the other hand, never settled for "good." Instead she and her wheelchair-bound husband headed out on their next adventure as soon as classes adjourned for summer. In the case of this African trip, Helen would take 1,600 feet of movie film, paint 14 large water colors, sketch dozens of scenes, and talk with scores of educators, and social welfare organizations—all to share the world with her students when the couple returned to Los Angeles that September. With the discovery of those films in USC's film archive, students today have the same opportunity at - *http://uschefnerarchive. com/project/baileyfilms/.*

She ignited a passion for exploration, investigation, and most importantly, service. In the same journal she expressed frustration with a the British system of education,

> *All East African education is keyed to the Cambridge entrance exams, and school authorities will adopt nothing new and practical for fear their graduates will not pass this exam. No passing, no high school diploma. British history, two years of Latin, rote-learned physics and chemistry without laboratory are required. The algebra and geometry taught has no connection with applied uses. All the native teachers have themselves passed this rigorous examination, and do not wish to see the system changed for its effect on their own prestige. Of 20,000 high school students in Uganda in 1960, 1200 took the exam and only 560 passed. Seems a hopeless rat race in an area where there is such a crying demand for practical education . . .*

Helen's travel journal provides insight from one of the many educators she met in Africa—Fulbright scholar Dr. Joe Hearn, history teacher from Los Angeles City College, "He is already concerned at the stiff British formality, the necessity of following a syllabus which the boys must learn by memory to pass the Cambridge Exams, and the lack of any practical education or democratic procedures."

When reminiscing about sitting in Helen's classes, never is there a mention of precise/technical/memorized information. What is always discussed are the slide shows, paintings, and movies which made the lessons come alive. Doc's classes provided what was relevant, but also a rare gift for young, poor American students—the development of a global vision combined with an expectation of upward mobility as a vehicle, not in service of greed, but in service to humanity.

In response, many of Helen's students have achieved illustrious careers in public service. When given a gift of the magnitude of "seeing" the whole world and witnessing an example of engagement with that world on the scale of a Helen Miller Bailey, her protégés found it impossible to avoid sharing that experience with others; many of Helen's students became educators.

The educator in me took a long time to surface like a diamond from miles within the earth. But I do try every day to encourage my students to ponder topics previously unknown to them or conditions which they never considered relevant to their lives. Some may share stories about my impassioned presentations in the years ahead. That will make an old soul very happy.

As with many challenging endeavors, "keeping the faith," as we used to say in the sixties, is often difficult. A teacher must believe that her "big ideas" will emerge from carefully orchestrated lesson plans. While rarely apparent in the classroom, we have to believe the important concepts will be translated into action at some critical point in our students' lives.

Helen Miller Bailey's legacy lives in the actions of those students who were influenced by her teaching, whether in a classroom or through community action. One of those men who hadn't been her student, or a guest in her home, serves as an excellent example of the scope of Helen's legacy.

Richard Alatorre

Los Angeles City Councilman

California State Assemblyman

Richard Alatorre didn't attend East Los Angeles College, nor were either of the Baileys ever his high school teacher. He did however experience Helen's broader impact on the community:

> *I met Dr. Bailey shortly after I was accepted to my choice of colleges. She was the treasurer of the Armando Castro Scholarship Fund and I was a 1961 recipient. I was very grateful for the much needed support and enjoyed meeting her. Later I came to know more about Dr. Bailey because many of my friends, and even my younger sister, were her students at ELAC. Helen Bailey had a tremendous impact on anyone who ever took her classes. She cared about the school, about the community college system and most importantly about the students.*
>
> *She worked tirelessly to promote the importance of the community college system. Through her own excellent teaching and the great professors she hired during her many years as a department head at ELAC, she made sure students never felt like it was some kind of "dumping ground." Indeed, all of my friends who attended ELAC, whether they transferred to four-year schools or not, all went on to excel in their chosen careers.*
>
> *Although I never attended community college I believe these schools provide the most important level of education in our state. During my time, the mission of the two-year schools was strictly to help students bridge the gap between*

high school and the four-year institutions. But now, not only do community colleges serve students in that way but very importantly through retraining, updating skills and preparing workers to change careers/professions when that becomes necessary, yet these schools remain the most underfunded in our system.

The irony is that although there are community colleges in every district in the State of California, because they are terminal institutions, there isn't the activism among students on campus to advocate for the resources comparable to the mission.

Helen's is a great human interest story in the context of how one person can make such a difference in another individual's life. And in her case you have to multiply these so many times over and over again. My recollection is that anybody who had her in class never forgot her. And each had a story—part of a lesson plan, a personal conversation, some coaching or coaxing, from Doc Bailey, which really impacted their thinking about the world.

Helen Bailey championed her students and our rich Latin American heritage. She even dressed in traditional Mexican clothing, which carried with it symbolism not lost on many. I can see her now as we speak, in that peasant blouse and bright green flowing skirt—she really had her own style.

Richard Alatorre followed his bachelor's degree from Cal State Los Angeles with a master's degree in Public Administration from the University of Southern California. Alatorre has taught at both Cal State University Long Beach and University of California, Irvine.

He was elected to the California State Assembly in 1972, where he served until 1983. He was the first Latino in twenty-three years to be elected to the Los Angeles City Council in 1985, a position he held until 1999. A pioneering politician, this "giver" is acknowledged as one of the architects of Latino empowerment in California.

Morle Bailey with students at Roosevelt High School

Helen Miller Bailey with art students at an East Los Angeles junior high school

Helen and Morle's mountain home in La Cañada, California,
where thousands of Eastside students visited

Guatemalan Village Scene,

Helen Miller Bailey

CHAPTER THIRTEEN

Doña Elena, Latin American Scholar

The air must have been warm and dry against her left cheek as she sped west down Third Street from her beloved East Los Angeles College toward Beverly Hills that autumn day in 1956. Helen surely loved those hot LA Santa Ana winds that blew off the Mojave Desert—a singular reminder of her Central Valley hometown.

Certainly, there was nothing near her parents' Modesto dairy farm like the Wilshire Ebell Club where she was headed that afternoon. Established in 1897 as the third women's social club in California, the club was named for German educator Adrian Ebell (1840–1877) who founded study groups in Europe and the United States for the purpose of providing educational opportunities for women, summarily denied higher education in those days. Members

225

opened the grand and current location on Wilshire Boulevard in 1927—seventy-seven thousand square feet of elegance dedicated to hosting classes, lectures, and service project planning sessions. The two thousand Wilshire Ebell members represented a great audience and donor pool for Helen's lectures on foreign lands and oil painting sales. While she may have been somewhat uncomfortable among "the ladies who lunch," Helen often responded to their invitations to lecture, armed with the colorful source of scholarship funds in tow.

Newspaper archives announce her lectures from 1934 through 1972 at the Ebell, the Southwest Museum, and the Beverly Hills Women's Club. Although she spoke about her African and European travels (such as her presentation of color films on Spain and Portugal at the silver anniversary of the Daughters of the American Revolution and the exhibit of her paintings at the Beverly Hills Women's Club in 1958), the majority of Helen's talks centered on Latin America: rural Mexico, the San Blas indigenous people of Panama, Guatemala, modern Maya Indians in Yucatan, and the Zapotec Indians of Tehuantepec, Mexico.

Did the wealthy women meeting at the Wilshire Ebell that August day consider themselves Helen's patrons? After all, between them, a few bank vice presidents, and dedicated colleagues, Helen sold nearly nine hundred paintings developed from *plein air* sketches and photographs she and Morle had taken on their annual summer trips abroad.

Perhaps they really loved her work; or, simply enjoyed the bragging rights from their philanthropic relationship with her, this lovely, young genius PhD USC alum teaching among the poor. Or, maybe they simply needed a reason to escape the boredom of their Hancock Park and Beverly Hills mansions.

Whether Helen was concerned with her audience's motives on this speaking engagement, or any other, is unknown. Likely what really mattered to her was replenishing the Armando Castro Memorial Scholarship Fund she had organized the year before. Fundraising might have been difficult the last few months due in part to the lingering effects of the economic recession of 1953.

She likely needed sales that afternoon; otherwise, how would her boys stick with their studies and fulfill the dreams she had for them? You see, if a student Helen had identified as a "giver" dare dream of transferring from community college to Cal State Los Angeles high up on the hill above the barrios, she'd drive them right past the Eastside toward the cool breezes of West Los Angeles to the more prestigious UCLA. If they had actually set their sights on UCLA, she'd shift their gaze to the real prize—Harvard. You see, some loftier goal could always be dreamed for "the givers."

After all, most of the students Helen supported were descendants of the mighty Aztecs. She made sure these high potential young men and women were introduced to their pre-Columbian ancestry. The pride in who they were as a people might help them look past the barrios of East Los Angeles. They might actually believe they were worthy of the superior educations needed to take their rightful place in society as college professors and social activists who would succeed her in the work of caring for the humanity of the Eastside.

Sometimes the difference between "the haves" at these luncheon events and "the have-nots" back at East Los Angeles College must have been almost unbearable for Helen Miller Bailey. The young people she nurtured through their first two years of college were not blessed with privilege of any kind. Selling her paintings to wealthy women was just one of the many ways she found to right the injustice of simply having been born on the wrong side of the river, which sliced Los Angeles in two—east versus west.

These differences, supported by a discriminatory education system, years later would be highlighted by Eastside students and their parents joining the "Walk Out" of 1968, which exposed the disparity between the inadequate Eastside school facilities and their superior Westside counterparts.

Today, more than half a century has passed since the first givers met her penetrating eyes, experienced her immense intellect, and accepted mentoring, financial support, and encouragement from Doc Bailey. They included young people from migrant farm worker camps, veterans returning to school after WWII and Korean Conflict, and those who made it back from the jungles of Vietnam, as bands of homeboys from Lincoln Heights, Maravilla, Boil Heights, and other LA barrios.

The givers honored Helen's teaching and took their places in service of the people:

> First Latino United States Ambassador
>
> Los Angeles City Council member
>
> California State Assembly persons
>
> Los Angeles County Supervisor
>
> Regional Director of Los Angeles County Probation
>   Department
>
> Mayor of El Monte, California
>
> Chair of the Civil Engineering Department at California
>   State University Los Angeles
>
> Provost California State University Los Angeles
>
> Civil rights lawyers
>
> Charitable foundation CEOs
>
> History and Business Professors
>
> K-12 Teachers and Reading Specialists

Chair of California's Democratic Party

Deputy California State Attorney General

CEO of the Corporation for Public Broadcasting

Co-Founder of *Telemundo* media network

Countless others in public service

The *Los Angeles Times* reported that Helen "dressed in colorful native Guatemalan costume presented a lecture on 'the Highlands of Guatemala' at the Southwest Museum at 3 p.m. November 6, 1972." That event was likely based on material from *The Latin Americans: Their Past and Present* (1972), which she wrote with her former student Frank Cruz.

Of Helen's six history textbooks, three were co-authored, including the comprehensive *Latin America, the Development of Its Civilization*, which she wrote in 1960 with San Diego State College History Professor Abraham Nasatir. Only two earlier texts by A. Curtis Wilgus (1931) and Salvador de Madariga (1947) are catalogued by the Library of Congress as subject matter dealing with the history of "Spanish-America."

Frank H. Cruz

Educator, Television Journalist, Entrepreneur

Telemundo Co-Founder

Former CEO Corporation for Public Broadcasting

USC Trustee Frank Cruz describes how one such textbook collaboration took place and its transformative impact on his life:

> *I approached Helen because I wanted to teach my high school students about the involvement of their*

Mexican ancestors here in the United States—how they got here—and give them a sense of their heritage. This information had been overlooked by traditional historians. When I had asked my colleagues where I could find such documentation, they said, "Nobody knows about that kind of history—why do you even want to pursue that?" Some were outright scornful of my interest.

So I went back to East Los Angeles College to my old professor and found her academically sensitive, helpful and encouraging; in fact, Doc's response was, "There is no such book available, so I guess we'll have to get together and write one!"

Even up to the early 1970s contributions of Mexican Americans were, to many academics, not subject matter that was valid. We went through a lot of that in those days. But hey—we didn't get dropped here from outer space. And if you look at the history of the Southwest, well, somebody wrote a constitution for California . . .

Ultimately the book did well for several years with the broadening awareness of teachers, especially if they had any Hispanic students in their classroom. While the monetary aspect had not been their goal, the royalty checks flowed in very nicely for some time. Helen used her share to replenish the student scholarship fund she managed at ELAC. They updated the text once after Cruz left teaching.

East Los Angeles College was primarily Hispanic and Japanese back in the sixties and many were first generation college students, first generation from immigrant parents. Cruz suggests that is one reason so many took a liking to Helen,

Somehow or another she believed in you and wanted to help you and supported you, which I guess if you had come from an educative process that was not very encouraging or perhaps because of lack of parental awareness, it was almost shocking to find someone like Helen to encourage you—it was very, very helpful. I felt it in my relationship to her.

In reaction to a lot of the turmoil that was going on at the campuses at that time, it was not uncommon to find polarized staff—traditionalists, hunkered down in their own academic wing—contending there was no legitimacy to ethnic studies, women's studies, and Chicano studies courses, which sprang up almost overnight along with these academic rifts. So in contrast, here was a female professor who was extremely open to legitimizing the field.

At the time it didn't even dawn on me the total significance of Helen saying, "Yes, let's do it together." The entrée—the background—a legitimate publisher— she was a writer at the university level. Yet she was willing to gamble on me. Because of the way she treated every one with dignity and respect and almost celebrated the fact that we were poor and faced challenges, it seemed she could identify something in your soul that could ignite your life's passion.

I've made many speeches over the years and usually Helen's unique support becomes a part of my talk. As recently as last week, I spoke to a Latina-oriented sorority at USC in my role as a trustee. I told them you must realize that one of your chores should be to mentor others, find people who need you to do what Doc Bailey did for so many. Let me give you an example—and I described how

*she made me believe I had the know-how, and the right, if
you will, to author a textbook.*

While he was working on a PhD and chairing the Chicano
Studies Department at Long Beach State, and due in large part to
his popular textbook, Professor Cruz was included when NBC-TV in
Los Angeles asked a group of professionals to put together a history
series on the Chicano in the United States. All fifteen or twenty were
teachers of Chicano studies or in positions of influence in the Los
Angeles area. Julian Nava recorded a segment on education, Fred
Sanchez prepared one on the zoot suits, Cruz contributed a piece on
Mexican immigration to the United States and served as the host for
the series. Viewers could earn credit at their community college by
writing a paper on one of the twenty one-half hour shows. The series
was part of what TV stations in those days called meeting public
interest obligations.

In 1971 the news director at ABC-TV called the professor, "Mr.
Cruz, are you interested in the news?" After Cruz replied that he was
a historian and a college professor, not a journalist, Bill Fyffe asked,
"Well, I would really like to meet you and fill you in on a transition
taking place at ABC." Veteran newsman Fyffe explained that the
network was bringing in lawyers to do TV consumer reporting,
meteorologists from university campuses to report on the weather,
and they wanted to bring in someone like him, a Spanish-speaking
professor, who was well-versed in the history of Southern California.

"I suppose," Cruz explained, "Helen would have appreciated my
thinking . . . I said to myself, if they want me to cover the subject
matter, at school I can get to 125 students a semester; if I do this, I can
reach thousands every day and that's how I got into KABC-TV News."

> *Up until then the television industry had been a pretty closed environment. Those who became sound men, camera men, producers or directors, or performed any function of the industry got the job primarily because they knew someone who helped them get into the union.*
>
> *So you can just imagine, all of a sudden management brought in a Latino and they thought who the hell is this guy? All five to eight reporters would go in early to ABC to begin to assemble their crew and get assignments. Every morning I'd over hear, "Oh no that Mexican reporter, I guess we've got to cover that damn thing in East LA." And then you'd have to convince the producer and director that the story you wanted to cover was important and had implications for the city as a whole.*

Cruz left KABC-TV and joined KNBC-TV where he spent ten years. He was the first Chicano television news anchor in Los Angeles. Covering the Hispanic community primarily, he met young civil rights lawyer Antonia Hernandez who described the evidence of unwanted sterilizations of women in Los Angeles County General Hospital. He reported a series of stories on their 1978 class action lawsuit, *Madrigal vs. Quilligan*, which he cites as one of the most memorable of the hundreds of stories and trials he covered in his television journalism career.

Based on undercover reporting for KNBC-TV in 1981, Cruz developed a five-part series covering the politics, the education, and the immigration issues of Latinos in Los Angeles. He was awarded an Emmy for that coverage.

Around 1983 Frank Cruz met Joe Wallach who had been head of the CBS-TV station in San Diego. CBS had transferred Joe a few years earlier to Brazil where he proceeded to create the largest network after NBC and ABC. After a few strategy sessions, Joe and his new partner Frank Cruz bought Channel 52, an independent TV station competing with KMEX in the Los Angeles market. The pair poured their hearts into the station with great results.

With the help of Reliance Capital Group out of New York they started buying other stations around the country. The amount of money Joe and Frank had borrowed was huge in 1985; thus, Cruz recalls fear was his motivator, "I was one of a group of nine who bought stations, spun off English speaking affiliates and purchased a large production facility in Puerto Rico. Eventually we had critical mass in the markets of the heaviest demographics for the Hispanic population in the country. *Telemundo* has gone through several iterations since I left in 1991."

President Bill Clinton appointed Frank Cruz to the board of the Corporation of Public Broadcasting; he served from 1991 through 2001 and was in his Washington DC office on September 11 that year. He was the first minority ever to chair the board, which is responsible for 1,000 public radio stations and 350 public television stations. Cruz is a trustee of University of Southern California and serves on the board of several organizations.

Frank Cruz reflected on Helen's mentorship, "Would my life have unfolded in such a rewarding fashion without Helen prompting me to write that much needed textbook, which positioned me as a published author of Southern California history? Your guess is as good as mine, but I know what my heart tells me."

Helen Miller Bailey with *Santa Cruz of the Etla Hills*, 1955

Wilshire Ebell,
Los Angeles
early 1900s

Professor Eugene Lazare and Doc Bailey during
one of her retirement activities

Praying Señorita
by Helen Miller Bailey

CHAPTER FOURTEEN
Working for Justice from the Grave

A connection between the work of eugenics proponents in America and Doc Bailey's lifelong commitment to an underserved population of young people in East Los Angeles, might seem an implausible result of this research; the connection found between the two was quite startling.

Recall from chapter 2 Terman's ideal of a meritocracy, run by those with the highest intellect, versus our democratic social/political structure. Then venture to the darkest implementation of that faulty science of eugenics. It is not difficult to imagine that a widely accepted goal of a quantifiable system of social order, organized by intelligence testing, could manifest tactics designed to reduce the number of humans deemed not worthy to serve the new order, as witnessed in Nazi Germany. Had the twisted tactics been left unfettered, such a society might well have resulted right here in America.

But the abuses/atrocities against humanity fueled by the goal of creating a master race had died with the fall of the Third Reich, right? Unfortunately, on a smaller, but no less sinister scale, interviews with five Bailey students coalesced around thousands of cases of unwanted sterilizations in California. The unsought connection began to emerge.

In 1973 Los Angeles County General Hospital medical resident intern Bernard Rosenfeld presented a report on sterilization abuse across the nation to the Los Angeles-based Center for Law and Justice where Antonia Hernandez, Helen's former student and friend, had just been hired out of UCLA law school. Rosenfeld presented notes from nearly two hundred medical charts supporting his claim that Mexican American women, and others, in Los Angeles County General's maternity ward, were unethically coerced by physicians and staff to agree to a sterilization procedure while experiencing multiple stressors of childbirth, language barriers, and sedation.

Rosenfeld recorded startling increases in *elective* hysterectomies and tubal ligations: 742 and 470 percent, respectively, from 1968 to 1970. As reported in the *American Journal of Public Health in 2005*, "according to Rosenfeld, County General obstetricians instructed resident interns to strong-arm vulnerable patients into accepting tubal ligations, often packaging the operation as a chance to gain needed surgical training (for the interns)."

How these tragedies could occur on such a large scale resulted from the confluence of public opinions, some sanctioned by law, all based in fear. In 1909 (coincidentally the year of Helen's birth), California was the third state to legalize the "asexualization" of patients and inmates, if such an operation would "improve their behavior." Influenced by the prevalent "science" of the day, State representatives bought into the faulty conclusions that physical and mental impairments, as well as degenerate behavior were inherited.

Passage of the sterilization laws was promoted by the state's secretary of the State Commission on Lunacy (renamed the Department of Institutions in 1921). These widely held beliefs were used to justify "improvement" of public health over protection of individual rights. Consider US Supreme Court Justice Oliver Wendell Holmes' 1927 *Buck v Bell* opinion affirming the constitutionality of sterilization in support of the collective health of the citizenry, "It is better for the world, if instead of waiting to execute degenerate offspring for crime, or to let them starve for their imbecility, society can prevent those who are manifestly unfit from continuing their kind."

California was a hub of the eugenics movement as it related to public health, guided by the Eugenics Section of the San Francisco-based Commonwealth Club of California and the Human Betterment Foundation in Pasadena. The latter offered the following leaflet from the late 1920s to the early 1940s:

EFFECTS OF EUGENIC STERILIZATION AS PRACTICED IN CALIFORNIA

- *One effect only—it prevents parenthood.*
- *It in no way or degree unsexes the patient.*
- *It in no way impairs the health of the patient.*
- *It is a protection, not a punishment; therefore, carries no stigma or humiliation.*
- *Patients and their families are among the best friends of sterilization. They know by experience what its protection means to them.*
- *It is approved by the medical staffs, social workers, probation and parole officers who have contacted patients before and after the operation.*
- *It permits many patients to return to their homes who would otherwise be confined in institutions for years. It thus prevents the break-up of families.*
- *It prevents the birth of children who would probably have a bad heredity, who could not be cared for properly, by their parents, and who would be likely to become state charges.*
- *It releases sterilized patients from confinement in state institutions, and leaves room for other waiting patients, thus increasing the efficient care for more defectives without increasing the cost to the tax-payer.*
- *It has not increased sex offenses; on the contrary, sterilized patients in California, for various reasons, chiefly educational discipline, show a great improvement over their former record of sex delinquency.*

- *It enables many handicapped persons to marry and to have a life normal in most respects, whose marriage without sterilization would be unwise if not disastrous.*
- *Conservatively and sympathetically administered, it is a practical, humane, and necessary step to prevent race deterioration.*

Note: California has had in effect since 1909, a sterilization law applying only to inmates of state institutions. Up to January 1, 1937, the state had sterilized under this law, 11,484 patients (5,933 males and 5,551 women). The Human Betterment Foundation has, for the past eleven years, been making an intensive study of the results to the patients, the family, and the community. For details:

The Human Betterment Foundation, 321 Pacific Southwest Building, Pasadena, California

The California law was amended twice in the 1950s and sterilizations declined initially. However, in the 1960s when President Johnson declared a War on Poverty, federal funds were newly-allocated to the states to subsidize birth control; the number of reproductive surgeries rose accordingly. Additionally, the new Medicaid program reimbursed physicians up to 90 percent for each sterilization surgery. When combined with the pervasive fear of overpopulation at the time, and a cultural loathing of welfare recipients, circumstances were ripe for widespread abuses throughout the United States, but nowhere as evident as in California where a reported twenty thousand nonconsented sterilizations were conducted (of the sixty thousand total in the United States).

Rosenfeld exposed chart notes such as these: "Emergency Cesarean section and sterilization . . . no consents signed—She wants to know type of operation done—Patient not asked about tubal ligation until after six hours, fifteen minutes of labor in hospital and after narcotics—The consent forms were written in English . . . patient speaks only Spanish."

Outraged by what she read in Dr. Rosenfeld's report, Antonia Hernandez took to the streets to locate Latinas who had been frightened into agreeing to tubal ligations, as well as those who were never actually informed that the surgery would be performed as part of a Caesarian section delivery.

Hernandez turned to many for help, the most effective of which came from Latina activists Olivia G. Rodriquez, Evelyn V. Martinez, and former Bailey student and future Los Angeles County Supervisor Gloria Molina. The three had formed *la Comisión Femenil Mexicana Nacionál* in an effort to advocate for Latinas' concerns over health, childcare, and other *familia* issues, which they regretted did not top the list of objectives of the fervent Chicano civil rights movement in California.

Because of the trust Molina and her colleagues had engendered in the community, lead litigator Hernandez was ultimately able to assemble a small group of brave women. Some of the women the three advocates spoke to did not even know they had been irreversibly sterilized. One of the ten female plaintiffs, Dolores Madrigal had consented to her sterilization surgery only after a medical assistant told her that her husband had already signed; he had not.

Hernandez and co-counsel Charles Nabarette at the Center for Law and Justice filed a class action lawsuit against the hospital's head of obstetrics and gynecology Dr. Edward James Quilligan.

The legal community's awareness was enhanced by the 1976 UCLA *Chicano Law Review* article, "Chicanas and the Issue of Involuntary Sterilization: Reforms Needed to Protect Informed Consent" co-authored by Antonia Hernandez and her colleague and friend Richard Avila. Another former student and protégé of Doc

Bailey's, Avila graduated later that year and went on to serve as deputy California attorney general, Health Quality Enforcement for twelve years.

In 1978 when *Madrigal v Quilligan* came before Federal District Judge Jesse Curtis, Hernandez was the lead litigator representing these, now barren, Mexican American women. Co-counsel Nabarette was the key author of the brief to the court. Richard Avila worked on supplemental briefs to Judge Curtis.

Hernandez and Avila had met in junior high school along with Antonia's close friend and Richard's future bride, Armida Torres. In 1967 they had all been active in the early days of the Mexican American Students Association (MASA) at East Los Angeles College. Perhaps the first Chicano college student group in California MASA was dedicated to the advancement of Chicanos. Helen was the faculty sponsor of the group.

As public awareness of the abuses emerged due to *La Comisión's* campaigning, the first and only Latino television news reporter of the day, Frank Cruz, had little trouble convincing his KABC-TV news editor Bill Fyffe that the entire trial should be covered. Unknown to Hernandez, Molina, or Avila, Cruz had not only been a devoted student of Helen but also had co-authored a Latin American history text with her in 1972. Cruz's coverage of court proceedings was enhanced by his delicate interviews with the plaintiffs who were, at the same time, courageous and humiliated (they would only agree to speak and be filmed with Cruz and his photographer seated behind them, lest their faces be identified.)

Despite affidavits from seven additional women and other corroborating testimony, Judge Curtis decided in favor of County General Hospital, "poor minority women in LA County were having too many babies; it was a strain on society; and it was good that they be sterilized." Alexandra Minna Stern writing for the *American Journal of Public Health* in 2005 summarized Judge Curtis's rationale, "relying on a simplistic interpretation of Mexican culture, suggested that if the plaintiffs had not been naturally inclined toward such large families, their post-partum sterilizations would have never congealed into a legal case."

Significant victories, however, did result. Procedures were changed requiring informed consent following a seventy-two-hour waiting period prior to sterilization operations.

Progress, yes—Justice, no—Helen's former students weren't finished with this case yet. In 1979, California State Assemblyman and Chairman of the Assembly's Health Committee Art Torres, former Bailey student (then representing the citizens in the service area of County General Hospital), introduced a bill to repeal the state's sterilization laws. Torres' bill was unanimously approved in the State Assembly and Senate and the law was repealed in 1983.

In 2008, University of Illinois Associate Professor Elena R. Gutiérrez, authored *Fertile Matters, the Politics of Mexican Origin Women's Reproduction*, detailing the Madrigal case, which helped a new generation comprehend the legal and social framework for a decades-old perspective on reproduction by Mexican American women. Gutiérrez concluded that such beliefs contributed to sanctioned sterilizations as the remedy to what had been considered a social problem.

Coincidentally, in 1961 Gutiérrez' father had been awarded an Armando Castro scholarship, which launched the academic career of Dr. Gutiérrez (see chapter 10).

So the connection is made between six exceptional individuals—each directly inspired by Helen Miller Bailey's teaching and generosity—whose independent relationships to her were unknown to one another, or at least obscured for the moment by their important work. Had Helen not died in 1976, she might have been the only person, until now, who could have grasped the irony of being studied as a Terman Kid and years later unknowingly guiding the demise of eugenics-inspired, government-sanctioned abuse, at least in California.

Antonia Hernandez
Civil Rights Activist
General Counsel MALDEF, Washington DC
CEO California Community Foundation, Los Angeles

Oh, yes, of course I remember Helen," responded Antonia Hernandez, "she was the chair of the Social Sciences Department at East Los Angeles College. I was a history major and she became my dear, dear friend. I became an attorney and actually helped her son Ted close Helen's estate. One of her paintings hung in my home for many years. She became my mentor. I visited her at both her La Cañada and Monterey Park homes. Helen was ahead of her time in so many ways. She wore those European sandals, what are they called? "Birkenstocks?" Yes, that's it. I thought they were awful. Who would know they would become so popular. She also loved to swim and did so every day—before Jane Fonda started a fitness craze.

It was because of Helen I planned to be a history teacher. I was accepted to Cal State Los Angeles and my dear friend Armida Torres (another Bailey mentee) encouraged me to try for UCLA. I did, and shortly after earning my teaching credential I decided I could contribute more on a different level and decided to become a lawyer.

People liked Helen. It was not so much her attitude, which was more assertive and demanding than sweet, rather, it was sharing her travel, exposing us to a wider world. She had a way of making you want to search out a significant life. Helen gave you a sense of your unique gifts and inspired you by her own enthusiasm to make a difference in the world.

The sixties was a turbulent time and we responded to people who emanated a positive view. She treated and viewed Latinos with respect. Guided by Helen, we would have the most interesting engagements back and forth in class. Everyone responded to her style in the classroom. Honestly I don't remember any other teachers other than one math teacher who reached out to me during all my academic career. These two were extroverts. This made it an easier connection between student and teacher. With Helen it was so natural. She had a few favorites. I suspect many of them will be interviewed for this book. We all flourished through her love, guidance, and high expectations.

She was such a complex person. She was the original sixties child, whilst chairing the department and carrying a vigorous speaking schedule with wealthy women's groups in search of student scholarship contributions. She was unorthodox up to the degree to which she had to maintain the social norms.

During these years I got very involved in the Chicano movement. My daddy would drive me to the picket lines and later in the day bring me my lunch. Culturally and socially many "unwritten rules" existed for a young

Mexican-American woman. But intellectually we could be anything we wanted to be as long as we followed the cultural norms. Looking back, I think Helen's formula for living was a strong model for me in that way, as I developed my community activism, which has been my life's passion.

I also took note of her relationship with her husband, which I viewed as a lovely partnership, the Ying and Yang of a productive marriage, if you will. His personality was more reflective and his wheelchair confinement caused him to be a somewhat reluctant participant in her aggressive schedule and yet he seemed to cooperate fully. She was the risk taker and adventure seeker. They travelled extensively, even though he couldn't always participate in all the activities. He took a great deal of pride in her accomplishments and the love in his eyes was evident anytime she walked into a room. After he passed away and she became ill with cancer again, I visited and read to her at her home in Monterey Park. The body was tired, but mentally Helen never aged.

Guided by the enforcers and nudgers in our lives, like our parents, Helen and good friends like Armida Torres Avila, all my siblings pursued professional careers and completed their college educations. My sister Mary teaches early childhood development at East Los Angeles College and our sister Lupe is a school principal. Maggie has been a teacher for 30 years.

If you were to ask me which person has been the greatest influence on my life, there are many who have encouraged and supported me, but in my heart, I know, Helen was it."

Antonia Hernandez is the is the President and Chief Operating Officer of the California Community Foundation, dedicated to improving underserved communities by strengthening the nonprofit sector through competitive grant making. She has been a civil rights activist and lawyer throughout her professional career, including president and general-counsel for the Mexican American Legal Defense and Educational Fund (MALDEF) in Washington DC; attorney for the East Los Angeles Center for Law and Justice; directing attorney of the Lincoln Heights office for the Legal Aid Foundation; and staff counsel to the United States Senate Judiciary Committee (from which she took a brief leave to coordinate Senator Ted Kennedy's Southwest campaign for Democratic presidential nomination).

Gloria Molina
Los Angeles County Supervisor
Civil Rights Activist

> *I was a little envious of day time students at East Los Angeles Junior College who seemed to have more access to the caring professors on campus, explained Supervisor Molina.*
>
> *While I took a full load of classes, they were at night to accommodate my family and work life. I do remember being mesmerized in Dr. Bailey's classes. Because I was a shy young woman at the time, Doc's energetic spirit, positive attitude, and eye contact were really great models of professional presence for me—I was fascinated. I have never met another professor like her since. Doc's personal passion for her students filled the space completely in her*

classroom. She made what we read about in our textbook come alive through all her firsthand knowledge about how people actually lived and worked in the places we studied. Her storytelling skills were amazing.

Helen Miller Bailey served as a type of role model few of us had in our lives. She was a woman of the world with such a commanding presence. She made you want to be somebody and she actually served as the pathway to significant work in service to our community and state. Though difficult to put into words, it was simply her way of being that helped me to open the door to my future.

Molina's future would prove to be a model for many Latinas. She first entered political life as chief deputy to both California State Assemblyman Art Torres and Assembly Speaker Willie Brown. She served in the Carter White House and the San Francisco Department of Health and Human Services. She was the first Latina to be elected to the California State Assembly and the Los Angeles City Council. In 1991 she similarly broke barriers on the Los Angeles County Board of Supervisors.

Her accomplishments as a county supervisor are numerous and represent a transformation of the board's focus on Eastside projects. Her early victory against the construction of a state prison in her district marked her as a force to be reckoned with and a fierce advocate for her constituents.

FROM BAILEY'S LOG CABIN

CHAPTER FIFTEEN
A Candle Burns Out, Lighting a Path for Others

Talking with retired professor Nora Jensen is a lively experience. Nora was hired by Helen in 1972 to teach political science at East Los Angeles College, a post she held for fifteen years. The two strong-willed women had their differences, "We had opposing ideas on many subjects but I think we got along well because our arguments were entertaining for each other." Nora and Helen had plenty of heated intellectual debates since philosophically Nora claims a much more liberal perspective. What is not debatable is that Nora proved to be a faithful friend, who spent many hours by Doc Bailey's bedside in the final months of her losing battle with cancer. The breast cancer treatment regimen of the day was crude, imprecise, and ultimately caused her death.

When asked what it was like to work with Helen, Nora explained that many in the Social Sciences Department at ELAC didn't like

Helen because of how she arranged their class schedules and what they described as the long-time department chair's general lack of organizational skills. Yet Bailey student Richard Avila recalls that in the late sixties the social science faculty lunched together nearly every day, as organized by Helen. Avila felt honored to have been asked several times to join the collegial group.

Nora's tone hardened, "Helen seemed proud that she wasn't bothered by petty annoyances; although, I got the idea that what she couldn't stomach were middle-of-the-roaders, people who didn't get fired up about *important* issues the way she did."

In response to how she thought Helen possibly had time to accomplish all the administrative tasks of a department chair while writing textbooks, travelling around the world, painting, running a scholarship foundation, caring for Morle, and teaching a full load of courses, Nora's voice warmed,

> *Helen found time for the important things. For instance, I was really flattered by Helen since she was really an iconic figure at the college and I was there at ELAC as an unknown and part-time teacher, yet Helen took notice of the special relationships I made with my students who would visit me in the department's office. Based on those observations, she made sure I got a full-time teaching post.*
>
> *In particular, I remember a student bringing in his drawings to my office. Helen mentioned to me later how effective I was in encouraging him to continue his education in architecture. I appreciated the moment she took to recognize me—I remember it like it was yesterday—she had that kind of effect on all of us.*

I think she did that a lot with people. She just knew
what a student or another teacher needed to hear to keep
them motivated. About ten years later, that student came
back to visit me at ELAC. By then he had become an
architect and was working for the State of California. The
appreciation he expressed was really very rewarding.

Chemo Guinea Pig

In the same year Nora began teaching full time and two years
before Helen was diagnosed with breast cancer, Helen and Morle
left their rustic mountain cabin in the foothills of the San Gabriel
Mountains, for a more traditional tract house located just two miles
from the ELAC campus in Monterey Park.

The drive down the mountain into East Los Angeles every
morning must have become somewhat taxing for Helen after so many
years. Since she was an avid swimmer, the new home's backyard pool
would not only mean no workday commute to speak of, but also just
as important, no daily drive to a local swim club for exercise.

Former students who read this account will undoubtedly
ask about the status of the cabin where over the years thousands
responded to Doc's end-of-semester invitation for hot dogs and
punch, camaraderie, and oral book reports. The cabin was a Sears
and Roebuck kit that Morle and "the Bailey Boys" assembled. A
skilled mason was hired to construct the large river rock fireplace
and chimney. The house was purchased from the Bailey estate in the
late 1970s by the current owner. While its acres of land have been
subdivided to accommodate additional homes, the cabin has been
preserved and is instantly recognizable, even to those who have not
visited the Baileys for nearly half a century.

Another likely motivation for the move was Morle's failing health. Eleven years Helen's senior, he was beginning to suffer from heart disease, perhaps related to being confined, by the ravages of polio, to a wheelchair for the last twenty years of his life. Day-to-day living must have been easier for Morle in the new house without the cabin's long dirt driveway, as well as more comforting to have Helen closer to him during the school week.

After Helen retired in June 1974, Nora visited often in that Monterey Park house while on breaks between her early morning and late afternoon classes (a schedule Helen had initiated years before). Helen's grandchildren fondly remember Grandma Doc's teacher friends who visited many times during her illness.

Richard Avila was a regular visitor. He recalls that although Helen remained an agnostic 'til the end, she often haltingly sang Protestant songs, while she accompanied herself on the piano, though breathing had become difficult.

Nora recalled Helen's deep concern, after her 1974 cancer diagnosis, that Morle (Petie, as she called him) would outlive her. Nora grimaced, "Helen and Morle were such lovers right up till the end that I had a hard time reconciling their behavior with her callous wish."

Morle cooperated, as he seemed to have done throughout their four decades of marriage, and succumbed ultimately to heart disease at age seventy-seven on June 30, 1975. Nora remembers that Helen was really quite relieved when Morle died. Helen's fear had been that Morle might outlive her as his main caregiver and not receive the quality of care she had been willing and able to provide.

Nora admitted developing a more empathetic understanding of Helen's feelings when, some twenty years later, Nora would care for her own husband during the last eight years of his life.

Nora had no empathy however, and expressed being quite annoyed, at her friend's obedience to a doctor's instruction to "Come back and see me in about year" after he had discovered a lump in Helen's breast. By the time Helen returned to his office, the cancer had spread, which began her demise over the next two years. Helen Miller Bailey died at age sixty-seven on September 9, 1976, in her Monterey Park home.

Nora and several contemporaries believe the Miller family upbringing as Christian Scientists, was what most likely influenced Helen's decision not to seek treatment earlier. As an atheist, Nora expressed disgust with what she viewed as unconscionable behavior, "Knowing her history and truly liking Helen, I just felt awfully sorry for her. In those days of early cancer treatment, she was having a horrid experience as a chemo therapy guinea pig." These treatments were in their infancy in the early seventies and no drugs were used to mitigate the ill effects of the mighty chemicals administered in the huge doses thought necessary.

Brains Over Brawn

"I really admired her strength professionally. Younger woman probably haven't experienced this kind of suffering," Nora began in our second phone call, "But Helen told me stories about the hostility she faced when applying for college-level teaching jobs among male-dominated faculty for a decade after completing her PhD at USC in 1934. One department chair expressed the sentiment of the times during Helen's interview, 'You will walk on my grave before I hire you,' a female as a college instructor—imagine!'"

Helen described, without rancor, her eventual success in biographical notes to one of her textbook publishers, "When the social sciences department chair position became available at East Los Angeles College in 1946, the selection was made based on a difficult testing competition." Perhaps to the administration's surprise, she scored the highest of the mostly male applicants and the job was hers—imagine!

Had it not been for this equalizing recruitment tool, Helen would likely not have been hired. Not only was she a woman, but also she was a married woman with children! For some context, the American Association of University Women reported that in 1920 only 12 percent of professional women were married. That number doubled by 1930, but remained decisively low especially if compared to the percentage of married male professionals. In 2014, these stats are difficult to imagine, but for perspective one needs to consider that it was not until 1970 top schools such as Princeton University of Virginia, and others opened their PhD programs to women. Women were represented in academia in 1940, but their participation declined after WWII from 27.7 percent in 1940 to 24.5 percent in 1950 and to just 22 percent in 1960.

During the post WWII years of 1945 to 1956 women were handicapped by the influx of males into academia. Indeed by 1956, over 2 million veterans had been educated under the GI Bill through community colleges alone. However, the sheer number of males entering higher education wasn't the only issue which caused the decline in women in higher education.

The cultural norms valued women's rightful place in the home and rewarded men's contributions (WWII) with a return to their rightful place in the professions. Just as had happened after WWI, women who had been needed to take on traditionally male roles in business and academia during the war years were then derailed into women's roles. The long-held view was that a liberal arts education would soon be sacrificed to marriage and child rearing. Most married women with PhDs were funneled into home economics departments regardless of their fields of study.

Most women acquiesced. Indeed, the American Council on Education reported women's lack of ambition outside of marriage as a social problem. Eventually a women's movement reminiscent of the nineteenth century suffragettes would turn "the problem" upside down. That was decades away from what Helen Miller Bailey, PhD, experienced between 1935 and 1946 as she pounded on higher education's door. The difference between 1920 and 1945 was that the doors were now open to women as students, albeit often grudgingly, but vocational success was now viewed by society as counterproductive to a harmonious family life, the responsibility of women.

So here we had our trailblazer with a genius IQ, a PhD, and a family who had supported herself since she was 17 by waiting tables, while attending Berkeley and then by teaching in high schools at twenty-two, who certainly wasn't interested in home economics. We can just imagine that a professional interview wouldn't have gone well. Although we do know that Helen could push right up against the social norms, she never went so far as to jeopardize her ability to contribute.

Describing her own experience with gender bias Nora added, "Even when I completed my second degree and was interviewing as a labor negotiator in the late 1960s, I became aware the committee simply did not believe a woman could do the job."

Nora ended our telephone conversation, "I worked really hard to live without guilt by doing what was the right and honorable thing, including being honest and speaking my mind." She said as she looks back she has no guilt about her relationship with Helen, "I stuck by her to the last days because I liked and admired her, and I think Helen enjoyed my visits."

What a dirty trick that Helen's life would be cut short, at sixty-seven, before she could witness the extraordinary careers of her "givers." She should have had the chance to express her joy when one of the earliest students at ELAC was appointed as the first Latino United States Ambassador to her beloved Mexico.

Dr. Julian Nava

US Ambassador to Mexico

History Professor Emeritus, California State University Northridge

President Los Angeles Board of Education

The newspaper accounts of Helen's retirement ceremony in 1974 all include comments by Dr. Julian Nava, former US ambassador and history professor emeritus at Cal State University at Northridge.

Julian Nava's journey from humble roots in East Los Angeles, his doctoral degree from Harvard, and illustrious career in education are emblematic of the American dream. One wonders if growing up in Boyle Heights, as in most sections of East Los Angeles, was both a curse and a blessing for one who would venture into public life. Breaching societal boundaries—being labeled "the first . . . "—requires uncommon courage and fortitude. Whereas understanding, and respecting cultural differences might come naturally to one schooled with Italians, Japanese, Armenians, Russians, Mexicans, Jews, Catholics, Russian Orthodox, and Protestants.

As a very young boy, Julian swept hair from the floor of his father's barbershop and played with scraps from Dad's woodshop out back. Julian has written of being inspired by his father's carving craftsmanship, which is perhaps why or how he later decided to make the frames himself for the pair of Helen's paintings hanging in his ranch house today.

The Great Depression hit the immigrant family hard and Julian's father lost his barbershop. The scarcity of jobs and the swelling rolls of families on Federal relief, combined with the proximity of Los Angeles to the Mexican border, and a prevailing anti-immigrant public mentality caused many Mexican American families in the early 1930s, to prepare to suffer "repatriation" to Mexico—yes, even the American born.

In a twist of fate, while his family waited for the train that would carry them south to Mexico, young Julian suffered a ruptured appendix. The family never left; rather; they attended to him during his two week hospital stay and relied on the charity of family members to get them back on their feet (having sold all furniture and household contents after being notified they were being "sent home").

Members of his family and neighbors worked at the huge Maravilla brickyard, then a countryside area called "miracle," which had quickly sprung up to house the immigrant workers.

Young Julian's father did construction work for the largest of President Roosevelt's New Deal agencies, the Works Progress Administration (WPA). Created in 1933, the WPA was responsible for creating 8,500,000 jobs between 1935 and 1943 (when the program was dissolved). One of the projects Señor Nava was assigned to was construction of the last grand train station to be built in the United States.

Union Station was erected on the very Downtown LA site where a train would have facilitated the family's return to Mexico a few years earlier. Even so, Julian says he looks fondly on that beautiful building whenever passing it while driving through Los Angeles. Financed by the Atchison, Topeka, and Santa Fe; Southern Pacific;

and Union Pacific railroads, the fusion of Spanish Mission and Art Deco architectures was completed in 1939. The iconic transportation complex would later facilitate the transport of thousands of US troops and serve as a major hub for defense workers arriving in California.

To supplement the family's meager, but sustaining income from the WPA, the Nava's spent many summers living in tents picking apricots in the Simi Valley; since, farm workers were in such short supply as the country geared up for WWII. Shortly after the war ended, Nava worked with labor leader Cesar Chavez to form the Community Service Organization in Los Angeles.

Although many Mexican American youth volunteered for military duty, their families were not welcomed in the great movie houses of downtown Los Angeles. And, as mentioned in chapter 1, Julian remembers that he and other Mexican American boys were not allowed to enter a local *public* swimming pool except on the day before the pool was cleaned.

Discrimination in the Navy by the last years of WWII was somewhat more subtle . . . Julian was designated ineligible for flight school because he had more than three cavities. But all in all, military service and subsequent GI benefits opened up the world to him and caused Julian to seek a college education at the newly organized East Los Angeles Junior College.

Any honorably discharged veteran who had served ninety days or had been injured in the line of duty was entitled to a free college education. The government would pay for tuition, books, and fees at any approved institution. California led the nation by opening eighteen new public junior colleges in the first five years after the GI Bill passage.

The community college system was in its way WWII's great gift to the country. Brave survivors of military service in all 50 states needed the skills to enter (or reenter) the workforce as well as the opportunity to complete their interrupted education; the country responded. Eventually, California would boast 110 community colleges where the focus remains on teaching expertise, vocational skills, and preparation for successful transfer to a four-year college. No one seeking an education is turned away.

Julian was elected student body president of East Los Angeles Junior College and formed a close relationship with his history professor, Doc Bailey. Dr. Nava remembers, "I decided to become a teacher due to the inspiration of one of my professors at "East," as we called East Los Angeles College. Helen Miller Bailey taught social sciences with great skill and inspiration. She took a special interest in Mexican Americans, advising us in many things and inviting many to her home in the mountains nearby. Her husband had been my physics teacher at Roosevelt High School, so I was almost one of her family. Doc, as we called her, was always there to lend you a few dollars for books or to scold you lovingly for not doing well."

Julian Nava's career includes being the first Latino to be elected to the Los Angeles City School Board where he served as president during a portion of his twelve-year post. He was appointed US Ambassador to Mexico in 1980. He directed the Los Angeles Children Art and Music School for two years, made an unsuccessful run in the Los Angeles mayoral race in 1993. That same year he served as a pallbearer at the funeral of Cesar Chavez. Dr. Nava retired with Professor Emeritus status from California State University Northridge in 2000.

In his biography, *My Mexican-American Journey*, Dr. Nava acknowledges how the inspiration he received from Dr. Bailey and his professors at Harvard played out in his own teaching career at Cal State University Northridge, "Just now a former student walked into my office to say hello. I feel good that he is a college teacher also. In a way, I have been reproducing myself and paying back the help others gave me along the road to college teaching."

In many ways Dr. Nava's statement sums up Helen Miller Bailey's life and teaching career. Far too soon, the candle burned out while lighting a path for others.

Visit *www.HelenMillerBaileyBio.com* to enter your own story of an inspirational teacher. Visit USC's Hefner Moving Images Archive at *http://uschefnerarchive.com/project/baileyfilms/* to view many short films the Baileys shot on their global adventures from 1934 to 1975.

Grandma Doc with Sputnik, Mary Alice, Maggie,
and Helen Lorraine (left to right)

ACKNOWLEDGMENTS

Without the support of many, this work would not have been possible. Most graciously, Helen's granddaughter, Mary Alice Bailey Welday, provided me total access to family photos and documents. She supported my efforts and celebrated any breakthroughs with such zeal. She has become a close friend.

Frank H. Cruz spent so many hours reciting his recollections of his old professor, attending readings from the manuscript, and introducing me to those who could help me finalize the project. I am deeply indebted to his kindness and support.

Similarly, I owe so much to all Helen's accomplished former students who generously told her story through recollections of their professor, mentor, and friend.

The support of librarians Choonhee Rhim and Erica Montenegro, at the Helen Miller Bailey Library at East Los Angeles College, never waned throughout this long process, even throughout Ms. Rhim's tremendous efforts during the renovation and rededication of the library in 2012.

The identification and preservation of Helen Miller Bailey's travel films is the work of archivists Dino Everett and Licia Marie Hurst at the USC SCA Hugh M. Hefner Moving Images Archive. Their generous collaboration with this work is greatly appreciated.

With ease and patience, book cover and website designer Pamela Meistrell's artistic and technical skill captured my vision for this California story.

Family and friends who cheered on the project were most important of all: Geoff Soza, Sunny Elizabeth and Douglas Grean, Richard and Armida Avila, Joel Busch and Kaori Tanegashima, Evelyn Joiner, Jennifer Muehlbach, Mary DePerine, Becky Hopkins, Linda Lee (LA), Lynda Lee (San Diego), Barbara VanSycle, and dear friends and manuscript readers Julie Hatoff, Cathy McAndrews, and Edward Pohlert.

APPENDIX A

STANFORD UNIVERSITY, STANFORD, CALIFORNIA 94305-2130
JORDAN HALL, BLDG. #420

ALBERT H. HASTORF
BENJAMIN SCOTT CROCKER PROFESSOR
IN HUMAN BIOLOGY AND
PROFESSOR OF PSYCHOLOGY, EMERITUS

PHONE: 415-725-2451
FAX: 415-725-5699
e-mail: hastorf@psych.stanford.edu

August 20, 2009

Dear Professor Soza,

I have your recent letter concerning the file on Helen Miller Bailey. Tracy Dow and I have talked about this some time ago. She has searched for the Bailey file carefully and its disappearance is a mystery to us all.

This study has a long history and there were directors and research associates well before me. I fear I cannot offer any explanation as to what happened. We do maintain tight security on the files. I'm very sorry about this glitch.

Sincerely,

Albert H. Hastor
Professor of Psychology, Emeritus

APPENDIX B

MASONIC HOMES
OF
CALIFORNIA

OFFICE OF THE ADMINISTRATOR

HOME FOR CHILDREN
20336 E. BADILLO
COVINA, CALIF. 91724

June 7, 1974

Dear Dr. Bailey:

"All hearts grow warmer in the presence
   of one who, seeking not his own,
Gave freely for the love of giving,
Nor reaped for self the harvest sown.

Thy greeting smile was pledge and prelude
Of generous deeds and kindly words;
In thy large heart were fair guest chambers
Open to sunrise and the birds."
            . . Whittier

Thanks for the many years of love, inspiration,
and joy!

James C. Blaine

22815 Costa Bella Dr.
El Toro, Ca. 92630
March 23, 1974.

Dear Mr. Lazare,

I was very much interested in hearing of your plans to
honor Dr. Helen Miller Bailey. She certainly more than deserves
recognition for her love, devotion, and service to her students
and the community throughout the years.

I can lay no claims to being a distinguished person, as
you mentioned in the letter, deserving of a place on a sponsoring
committee to honor Dr. Bailey, but, as an old friend, I certainly
would like to attend any functions given in her honor and contribute to a fund to help her dreams come true.

Although we have not been in close touch for many years,
I have always regarded Helen as a very special friend. Our acquaintance began in a small boarding house near the University of Califo-
nia campus. I was instantly drawn to this vivacious, dynamic, dedicated student with so many interests and talents. She really helped
me over many a rough spot in my first experience of being far from
home. I remember waiting up nights until she was through at her
work as a waitress which she held to put herself through the University. Just to chat awhile with her was the bright spot in my day.
She arranged a birthday celebration for me, took me to visit interesting friends, and invited me to her home in Modesto on several
occasions where I enjoyed her family's wonderful hospitality.

After she began teaching in Southern California, she
introduced me to the All Nations Foundation in Los Angeles where
she was already doing social service work, and I did some volunteer work in the Day Nursery there. My association with the director
Arilita Roberts led to my future employment under her at the Assistance League in Hollywood which sponsored a Day Nursery for working
mothers' children.

Otto and I were very pleased to attend the exhibition of
Helen's paintings held at East Los Angeles College some years ago
and to have an opportunity to catch up on some of the many years in
between with her and her husband, Morle, whom we also regard as a
very dear friend. Speaking of her paintings, I have treasured
these many years a painting she made for me, one of her first oil
paintings, of the tower on the Berkeley Campus. It brings back
many memories.

Thank you for this honor and a chance to relive some of
these treasured memories.

Sincerely,

Ethel Bottenberg

CITY OF LOS ANGELES
CALIFORNIA

TOM BRADLEY
MAYOR

JEROME F. MILLER
DIRECTOR

BARBARA A. BELL
ASSISTANT DIRECTOR

MAYOR'S
**OFFICE OF
URBAN DEVELOPMENT**
ROOM 1400
CITY HALL
LOS ANGELES 90012
485-3406

April 2, 1974

Dr. Helen M. Bailey
East Los Angeles College
5357 East Brooklyn Avenue
Los Angeles, California 90022

Dear Dr. Bailey:

How can I ever start my sincerest thanks for giving me my first start in my career in life when I first graduated from high school.

It was you who inspired me to continue my education and assured me that even though there would be disillusions, heartbreak and obstacles in my way, I should never get discouraged, but keep on smiling and thinking positive and always help my fellow man. This way I would always be a happier person in spite of all encounters I might have. For that alone, I am very grateful and very happy. I will always treasure that inspiration and try to continue to live the rest of my life with a clear mind.

Sinceramente, su amiga

ALVINA C. CARRILLO
Project Coordinator

ACC:vm

36 Aurora Drive
Rolling Hills Estates
April 3,1974

Mr.Gene Lazare,Executive Secretary
Committee to honor Helen M.Bailey
EAst Los Angeles College
Los Angeles,California

Dear Mr.Lazare:

I feel honored by being asked to join in recognizing
Dr.Helen Miller Bailey. I am enclosing a check of
$100.00 for the scholarship fund in her name.

Personally I did not have much contact with Dr.Bailey.
I had long known that she was one of the children who
were rated in the genius class,and of some of the others
whom I have known as adults I have felt that Dr.Bailey
has demonstrated the most talent and the greatest concern for humanity. Your letter adds to my knowledge of
her.

My own personal gratitude to her came in in 1955 when
she hired my daughter as a member of her staff. At that
time Dr.Bailey proved that she was years ahead of civil-
rights which protects the rights of equality as to sex.
Dr.Condon had taken the examinations for a college position in the city school system for several years and following each test she would receive a letter explaining that
although her score was very high the colleges were not
hiring women. Finally she was placed on the list and Dr.Bailey
did not discriminate against her either as to sex or her
religion (catholic). Teaching under Dr.Bailey was a joy for
Mary and when she left in 1963 it was only because of the
greater opportunities as a professor at the University
of San Jose (then California State College-San Jose.)

While my daughter was teaching in ELAC each year Dr.Bailey
encouraged my daughter to have a member of the social work
profession present a program on the opportunities for a
professional social worker,particularly spanish speaking
Mexican Americans.

I have had at least on two occasions, a speaker for one
of my own programs (AAUW) who had been helped through college by the Armando Castro Fund. I felt personal pride in
the favorable reactions to a good speaker.

Personally I feel no honor can be great enough for this
gifted artist and humanitarian.

                          Sincerely,

                          Elisabeth C. Condon

[Dr. Mary Condon died in 1971, at age fifty-five. The History Department
at San Jose State University established a memorial book fund in her honor,
which continues to purchase Irish history and British imperialism works,
Dr. Condon's areas of expertise.]

Mr. Lazare:

MESSAGE FROM MEXICO CITY PHONED IN THIS MORNING
TO BE READ AT THE BANQUET

Dear teacher of mine:

From Mexico City I send you these words, my best
congratulations on your retirement. You have not only
been my best teacher in 1930, but acted like a mother to me
many times afterwards.I had beautiful months in Mexico in
1933 and in 1954 acting as guide and son for you and for
Dad Bailey. Now we greatly thank you for sending one of my
daughters Elsa to secondary school in Mexico City. I am so
glad you kept in touch always, for I have followed your advice
ever since. From my heart your compadre in Mexico City,

Ricardo Mercade Garcia

BOARD OF SUPERVISORS
COUNTY OF LOS ANGELES
821 HALL OF ADMINISTRATION / LOS ANGELES, CALIFORNIA 90012

ERNEST E. DEBS
SUPERVISOR, THIRD DISTRICT

April 11, 1974

Mr. Gene Lazare, Executive-Secretary
Committee to Honor Helen M. Bailey
East Los Angeles College
5357 East Brooklyn Avenue
Los Angeles, California 90022

Dear Mr. Lazare:

I am pleased to submit these few sentiments regarding
Dr. Helen Miller Bailey.

From the outset when she appeared on the scene at East
Los Angeles College in the early days when ELAC was located
in the west wing of Garfield High School, I appreciated La
Señora's interest and dedication to those few of us who were
fortunate to have had the opportunity to pick up our education
where we left off because of World War II.

Dr. Bailey in my estimation represented those instructors
who not only were extremely capable but who went beyond and
added an important human ingredient so essential to moving the
student beyond mediocrity.

Señora, my very best wishes for continued health and
success.

Sincerely,

ERNEST E. DEBS

ARNOLD MARTINEZ
Assistant Chief Deputy

EED:AM:sj

community planning & development corporation

March 25, 1974

Dr. Helen Miller Bailey
EAST LOS ANGELES COLLEGE
5357 East Brooklyn Avenue
Los Angeles, California 90022

Dear Dr. Bailey:

I take this occasion to express my gratitude to you for the
tremendous encouragement and inspiration that you gave to me
and to many other youth in this community. I have never forgotten you nor will I ever.

With love and appreciation,

XAVIER MENDOZA
Executive Vice President

XM:br

BOARD OF SUPERVISORS
COUNTY OF LOS ANGELES
383 HALL OF ADMINISTRATION / LOS ANGELES, CALIFORNIA 90012

JAMES S. MIZE, EXECUTIVE OFFICER
RICHARD A. SCHOENI, ASST. EXEC. OFFICER
(213) 974-1411

November 9, 1976

Mr. Eugene Lazare
Social Science Department
East Los Angeles College
5357 East Brooklyn Avenue
Los Angeles, California 90022

Dear Mr. Lazare:

On motion of Supervisor Edmund D. Edelman, the Board of

Supervisors is sending you the enclosed memorial of its

adjournment on October 26, 1976, as an expression of

deepest sympathy.

Very truly yours,

JAMES S. MIZE

Enclosure

UNITED NATIONS ASSOCIATION of the UNITED STATES OF AMERICA

SOUTHERN CALIFORNIA STATE COUNCIL

MAY 15, 1974

DEAR HELEN!

"... THE BEST IS YET TO BE, THE LAST OF LIFE FOR WHICH THE FIRST WAS PLANNED...."

NOW YOU CAN HAVE EVEN MORE FREEDOM TO PURSUE THE MANY CREATIVE ENDEAVORS WHICH HAVE SO CHARACTERIZED YOUR BEAUTIFUL LIFE.

AT A TIME LIKE THIS MEMORIES COME STREAKING BACK OF THE HAPPY TIMES WE HAVE BEEN PRIVILEGED TO SHARE TOGETHER UNESCO CONFERENCE IN SAN FRANCISCO, CURRICULUM ADVISORY COMMITTEE MEETINGS AND THE LUNCHES AFTERWARDS IN THE OLD COFETERIA, SPECIAL EVENTS AT THE COLLEGE WITH YOU AND MORLEY IN THERE PITCHING. BUT ABOVE ALL THE MANY YOUNG PEOPLE WHO HAVE SAID TO ME, "OF COURSE I KNOW DR. BAILEY — IS THERE ANYONE WHO DOESN'T?" THIS WOULD BE FOLLOWED BY A RADIANT SMILE AND A GLOWING ACCOUNT OF HOW YOU HAD HELPED THAT INDIVIDUAL TO KNOW AND BELIEVE IN HIM OR HERSELF AND THEN TO FIND EXCITING DOORS THROUGH WHICH THEY COULD GO TO MAKE A LIVING BUT MORE THAN THAT, LIVING CONTRIBUTION TO THE UN MET NEEDS OF MANKIND

AS YOU KNOW I WAS PRIVILEGED TO PLAY A SMALL PART IN THE ELIMINATION OF MORE THAN TWENTY FIVE SCHOOLS FOR SEGREGATED MEXICAN-AMERICAN YOUTH IN THE EASTERN SECTION OF LOS ANGELES COUNTY, RIGHT AFTER THE SECOND WORLD WAR. SO MANY OF THE YOUTH WHO AVOIDED THIS CRIPPLING EXPERIENCE WERE FORTUNATE IN COMING UNDER YOUR LOVE AND INSPIRATION. I LATER HAD THE PRIVILEGE OF HAVING AS CO-WORKERS SEVERAL OF THOSE WHO SANG YOUR PRAISES. PERHAPS WE CAN NOW FIND SOME OPPORTUNITY TO INITIATE SOME CREATIVE COMMUNITY PROJECTS WITH THESE FINE YOUNG PEOPLE THAT WILL GIVE US ALL A "NEW BIRTH OF FREEDOM."

LOVE

Dwight

[At a time like this memories come streaming back . . . but above all the many young people who have said to me, "of course I know Dr. Bailey—Is there anyone who doesn't?" This would be followed by a radiant smile and a glowing account of how you had helped that individual to know and believe in him or herself and then to find exciting doors through which . . . {they could} make a contribution to the unmet needs of mankind . . .]

BOARD OF TRUSTEES
2140 WEST OLYMPIC BOULEVARD, SUITE 310 / LOS ANGELES, CALIFORNIA 90006

May 6, 1974

Dr. Helen Miller Bailey
Professor of History
East Los Angeles College

Dear Helen:

It is with deep personal pleasure that I join your legion
of friends in saying thank you for your outstanding service
to humankind and to wish you a pleasant and productive
retirement.

It seems so many years ago that I drew inspiration from you
when Mary Tinglof and I were candidates for the Unified Board
of Education in 1957. I remember with gratitude your counsel
and encouragement.

Tell me, are you really sure you wish to retire? How about it
if we find a college presidency for you? You'd be great!

With respect and affection, I am

Sincerely,

Ralph Richardson
Member
Board of Trustees

RR:sh

COUNTY OF LOS ANGELES

OFFICE OF THE DISTRICT ATTORNEY
CRIMINAL COURTS BUILDING
210 WEST TEMPLE STREET
LOS ANGELES, CALIFORNIA 90012

JOSEPH P. BUSCH, DISTRICT ATTORNEY
JOHN E. HOWARD, CHIEF DEPUTY DISTRICT ATTORNEY
GORDON JACOBSON, ASSISTANT DISTRICT ATTORNEY

974-3531

April 18, 1974

Dear Dr. Helen Bailey:

You probably do not remember me because I was one of your quiet students. Nonetheless, I still learned alot from you during the two semesters in which you were my history instructor. Not only did you teach me about world history, you taught me about life itself, and this I feel was more important.

You stressed, I remember, the importance of acquiring a good education, and this proved to be a significant turning point in my life. You used to frighten me a great deal many times by reminding the class that if we felt that the classes at East Los Angeles College were difficult, then a four-year college or university was really going to be tough. Even though you did frighten me, you really were preparing me; and as usual you were right -- it was tough.

My only regret is that I was too quiet in your classes; and because of this, we did not know each other better and this is my misfortune. I wish you the best of everything and I know you will enjoy yourself tremendously.

Sincerely,

Fred V Sainz

FRED V. SAINZ
Field Deputy

cv

June 1974

We all owe her so much, Chicano—non-Chicanos—everybody. But I owe her a special word of thanks for helping me to keep my sense of social purpose together; she made clear why I, a Chicano, was in school and what I owed my community.

Many years ago Manuel Santana and I organized a special class, which you may remember, through which we recruited Chicanos for ELAJC. This was around 1948, I believe. It now seems incredible that we had to work so hard, but Dr. Bailey sponsored us.

Chicanos, Blacks, and others who are born outside of privilege and luxury owe a great deal to instructors like Helen Miller Bailey, who came to areas of poverty with a kind of missionary zeal, to help the less fortunate. Long before educational opportunity programs were known, Helen Miller Bailey was pushing la raza into higher education.

With great gratitude,
Ralph Guzman, PhD
Merrill College
University of California Santa Cruz

The following excerpt from Professor David Sweet's 1988 Dr. Ralph Guzman In Memoriam is reprinted with the permission of the University of California Academic Senate.

Professor Ralph C. Guzman of the Boards of Study in Politics and Community Studies at University of California Santa Cruz died . . . on October 10, 1985. He was only sixty.

Ralph Guzman . . . was an influential participant in the Mexican-American struggle for a place in the sun. He lived on terms of intimate familiarity with both poverty and prosperity, failure and success, bitter humiliation and savored prestige . . . When most other educated Mexican-Americans were opting for assimilation into an admittedly inhospitable North American society, he chose the path of a hopeful but determined public advocacy of political and cultural pluralism—of a society which would respect the rights (and fast-growing numbers) of the Chicano community, while at the same time allowing itself to be enriched by the culture and values, as it had already been enriched by the labor, of Mexican immigrants like himself . . . He served with distinction in the Merchant Marine and Navy during World War II, participating in the final assault on Okinawa, and returned to complete an A. A. at East Los Angeles Junior College under the G. I. Bill in 1949.

During the 1950s, Ralph Guzman contributed substantially to the political mobilization of the Los Angeles barrio as an organizer for the Community Service Organization (CSO), crusading reporter and editorialist for the Eastside Sun and the Los Angeles Free Press, and close associate . . . of Congressman Edward R. Roybal and progressive journalist Carey McWilliams . . . In the early 1960s, before the Chicano power movement, he was a leading spokesperson for the Mexican-American community nationwide, and a vigorous supporter of Cesar Chavez and the Farm Workers' Union.

It was in this context that Ralph Guzman decided in mid-life to pursue an education for service as a scholar-activist and university professor. He completed his BA (1958) and MA (1960) in political science at Cal State Los Angeles and served for three years as Associate Director of the Peace Corps contingents in Venezuela and Peru, and returned home to become one of the few Chicano graduate students (and first to receive a Ph.D. in political science) at UCLA.

Ralph Guzman first taught at Cal State Los Angeles, and Mt. St. Mary's College, but in 1969 he was invited . . . to join the politics faculty and help build programs for minority students at the new University of California campus in Santa Cruz. There he was a co-founder of Oakes College and later Provost of Merrill College, a contributor to the Educational Opportunity Program, the Latin American Studies Program, the Third World Teaching Resource Center and the Merrill Field Program for Experiential Learning, and a very popular teacher . . . .

Late in the Carter administration, Professor Guzman served two years in Washington as Deputy Assistant Secretary of State of Latin America (the highest position yet attained by a Hispanic in the Department of State.

Professor David Sweet

CHAPTER NOTES

These notes describe the main sources used to compose each chapter and are provided for readers who are interested in research on the various topics.

Chapter One
Tarnish on the Golden State

Personal accounts of discrimination were compiled from personal conversations with Joe Perez, Dr. Julian Nava, and Manuel Lemus. Alejandro Morales's historical fiction *The Brick People* (1992) was used to understand the history of my own childhood neighborhood, my friends and classmates.

Sixty-five pages of an eighty-five-page paper Helen titled "East Los Angeles College History 1945–1974" was provided to me by her namesake library. She must have undertaken the project immediately after her retirement as she lists her title as, "Social Science Department Chairman, Emeritus." This document is the basis for my information on the early years of the college.

Information presented about California politician Richard Alatorre was obtained from a lengthy telephone interview with him as well as from former *Los Angeles Times* City-County Bureau Chief Bill Boyarsky's October 22, 1989, article, "Crossover Dreams."

Dr. Francisco E. Balderrama and Raymond Rodriquez's 1995 *Decade of Betrayal: Mexican Repatriation in the 1930s* (1995) in addition to overviews of *Immigration and Naturalization Service* by historian Marian L. Smith and Harvard University's Open Collections program's *Immigration to the United States 1789 to 1930* formed the basis for the paragraphs regarding US immigration policy relative to people of Mexican ancestry. Another source was the *USA Today* report of California State's January 2006 apology to two million deportees and their families, after passing the bill sponsored by State Senator Joe Dunn (D-Garden Grove).

As noted, in addition to several conversations with Dr. Nava, his autobiography, "My Mexican-American Journey," informed this chapter.

Chapter Two
A Modesto Termite Flies South to Los Angeles

Helen's participation in Lewis Terman's longitudinal study of California children with genius-level IQ scores was made known to me in a telephone interview with psychology professor Dr. Phyllis Woodworth and later confirmed by Stanford Psychology Professor Emeritus Al Hasdorf on the phone and in a letter. Understanding the background and motivation for the study was obtained from two articles in the July/August 2000 edition of *Stanford* magazine and University of North Carolina Population Center on-line article, "The Lewis Terman Study at Stanford University." Details of the security measures surrounding participant data were provided during two telephone interviews with Stanford University professor and science writer Joel N. Shurkin, as well as from his book, *Terman's Kids, the Groundbreaking Study of How the Gifted Grow Up.*

Information about the 1905 paper of French researchers Alfred Binet and Theodore Simon, titled "New Methods for the Diagnosis of the Intellectual Level of Subnormals," was derived from a 1998 introduction to their work by Henry L. Minton, University of Windsor. Minton's summary was compiled in an academic Internet resource, "Classics in the History of Psychology," developed by Christopher D. Green, at York University, in Toronto, Canada.

Information about Jess Oppenheimer's participation in Terman's study was obtained from Mitchell Leslie's 2012 article, "A Tale of Two Termites," for *Stanford* magazine.

Chapter Three
Helen's Letters Home: 1931 Steamship to China

The material for this chapter came from two handwritten letters from Helen to her parents from China in July 1931. The information about the 1931 China flood came from the National Oceanic and Atmospheric Administration's Internet news source www.noaanewsonline.

Chapter Four
Settlement House Work Builds a Foundation: From Revolution to Institution

The basis for this story was provided by Pasadena City College Professor Alberto Juarez Jr. during two telephone interviews in 2006 and 2014. Family information was confirmed with Dr. Desdemona Cardoza, former dean of social sciences at Cal State University Los

Angeles along with a phone interview with her mother Minna Cardoza-Dyer. Context, as well as statistics, was gleaned from historian Ken Starr's 2007 *California a History* and Patrick D. Lukens's 2012 *A Quiet Victory for Latino Rights*.

Other details were derived from several meetings with former Bailey student and ELAC Counselor Armida Torres Avila. *Movimiento Estudiantil Chicano de Aztlan* (MECHA)'s website, *www.nationalmecha.org* was very helpful in understanding the national coordination of the Chicano Movement in America.

Chapter Five
A-Wheel in Europe: 1936 Journal Excerpts

This chapter consists of excerpts from Helen's seventy-six-page journal, A-Wheel in Europe: 1936. History Professor Joel Busch assisted with German spellings and placing Helen's trip in context politically.

Chapter Six
Since a Family Wasn't Going to Come to Us . . . the Story of the Bailey Boys

Bruce Morle Bailey was interviewed by phone several times between 2006 and 2008 for this chapter. Mary Alice Welday-Bailey provided me with family photo albums, which had been captioned and dated by Helen.

Statistics regarding child welfare issues were obtained from the website of the US Department of Housing and Urban Development, which provides a history of the "orphan trains," the Labor Department's Children's Bureau and child welfare services under the Social Security Act. Legal nuances were derived from Rebecca S. Trammel's spring 2009 article in American University's *the Modern American.*

Excerpts were also taken from the Bailey's local paper, the *La Cañada Valley Sun*, May 6, 1954, article featuring the family.

Chapter Seven
The Revolutionary Promise of Rural Education: Mexico, 1934–1944

For the current state of literacy in Mexico I consulted UNICEF's website and *Report by Country* for 2013. Helen's travel journal, *Adventures in Mexico Volume V 1944* together with her sociological study of the Oaxacan hill town, *Santa Cruz of the Etla Hills* were the major sources of context for this chapter.

Chapter Eight
Blazing a Trail from Hicks Camp to College

A majority of the material for this chapter was obtained through interviews in El Monte, California, with former Mayor Ernie Gutiérrez, Richard Perez, and Dr. Ben Campos and information gleaned from the museum's website: *www.lahistoriasociety.org.*

I spoke to Jason Kosareff on the phone regarding his obituary of Father Coffield in the San Gabriel Tribune on February 21, 2005. I also purchased a copy of the priest's memoir, "Juanote" (January 2000), and read his 1974 letter to Helen.

Chapter Nine
A Life Defined: Before and After Macchu Picchu, 1947 Journal Excerpts

This chapter is composed entirely of excerpts from the 1947 Bailey travel journal, "South American Series, West Coast," made available to me by the Bailey family.

Chapter Ten
Monument to a Young Man

My search for information on the origins of the Armando Castro Scholarship Fund began at Los Angeles' Central Library wherein I easily accessed the *Los Angeles Times'* historical archive providing all editions of the paper from 1881 through 1990. In addition to the 1956 announcement of the KABC-TV airing of the DuPoint Cavalcade Theater presentation of "Monument to a Young Man," the *Times* reported the California State Controller aid to the Armando Castro Scholarship Fund on January 18, 1962. I also conducted telephone interviews with Daniel Garcia in Washington DC, Art Torres in Sacramento, California, and Lou Moret in Los Angeles. Dr. Gutiérrez was interviewed in his office at USC's Annenberg School of Communication and Journalism. Helen's papers loaned to me by the family contained her last will and testament.

Chapter Eleven
The Postcolonial Promise of Rural Education: Africa 1962 Journal Excerpts

This chapter consists entirely of Helen's travel journal, *the Adventuresome Baileys: Africa 1962.*

Chapter Twelve
Light My Fire, a Student's Memoir

My own 1970 classroom experience in Helen's World Civilization I and II courses at East Los Angeles College and the suggested reading of Alan Paton's *Cry, the Beloved Country* (1955) informed most of this chapter. The PBS *Frontline* report, "Diamond Empire," which originally aired in 1994 served to fill in some context and confirm my recollections as did the Arkansas Historic Preservation Program's Website and Steven Labaton's July 9, 2004, article for the *New York Times.* I collected information about the Diamond Crater State Park from its website.

I conducted a lengthy telephone interview with Richard Alatorre wherein he contributed his recollections of Dr. Bailey and his receipt of an Armando Castro Scholarship.

Chapter Thirteen
Doña Elena, Latin American Scholar

This chapter was prompted by the many news reports in the *Los Angeles Times* from 1935 through 1975. Additionally, I met with Frank Cruz near his home, at MiraCosta College where he spoke to first-time college students, and at USC where we viewed the Bailey films in the university's Hefner Moving Images Archive.

Chapter Fourteen
Working for Justice from the Grace

The motivation for this chapter arose from 2011 interviews with Frank Cruz, Felix Gutiérrez, Antonia Hernandez and Richard Avila, as well as my interview with Gloria Molina in 2012. Frank Cruz has become a great supporter of this work and shared many stories with me and students at both East Los Angeles College and MiraCosta College, where I teach.

Similarly Richard and Armida Avila have been spiritual advisors, of sorts, providing context and first-hand knowledge for this chapter and the entire project. We have met several times in Los Angeles and at my home in San Diego.

More details for chapter 14 were obtained from the 1978 Ninth Circuit US District Court case *Madrigal v Quilligan* No. 75-2057. Additional scholarly work referenced included: Rebecca Marie Kluchin's *Fit to Be Tied: Sterilization and Reproductive Rights in America, 1950–1980*; Dr. Alexandra Minna Stern's article for the *American Journal of Public Health* (July 2005), "Sterilized in the Name of Public Health, Race, Immigration, and Reproductive Control in Modern California;" Elena R. Gutiérrez's text for University of Texas Press (2008), *Fertile Matters, the Politics of Mexican-Origin Women's Reproduction*; and Franziska Castillo's article for *Latina* (September 2005), "Did These Women Save Your Life?" as well as Anne-Emanuelle Bir, and Natalia Molina's *American Journal of Public Health* article (July 2005*)* "In the Name of Public Health."

Chapter Fifteen
A Candle Burns Out Lighting a Path for Others

My phone interview with Nora Jensen was conducted in 2006. She was in her home in Novato, California. I first interviewed Dr. Julian Nava in 2007 in Escondido, California, and at that time he gave me a copy of his memoir, *Julian Nava: My Mexican American Journey* (2002). We have subsequently talked on multiple occasions.

I read Claudia Goldin's *Understanding the Gender Gap: An Economic History of American Women* (1990), and *America's Community Colleges: The First Century* (1994) by Allen A. Witt, James L. Wattenbarger, James F. Gollattscheck, and Joseph E. Suppinger. Also very helpful was Barbara Miller Solomon's *In the Company of Educated Women* for Yale University Press (1985).

INDEX

CHAPTER ONE
Reading Group Guide

What role does fear play in one group's ability to subjugate another? Have you experienced or witnessed attitudes and biases that influence behavior today that is not unlike the examples of discrimination described in chapter 1? What was your reaction? Are you proud of your behavior?

As a citizen of the world, can you identify conditions in other countries that resemble the United States of the early 1900s. Imagine, if you can, what our society might look like had President Lyndon B. Johnson been unable to gain support for the Civil Rights Act of 1964. How might your family have been affected?

Shifting Ideas to Action

Knowledge is often an effective antidote to fear. Consider gaining first-hand knowledge of other areas of your town or state: visit other religious institutions; attend a variety of public gatherings; enjoy ethnic festivals; attend city council meetings; explore diverse media sources, learn a foreign language, read ethnic-oriented literature, enroll in an ethnic studies course at your local community college; and most simply—talk with people who don't look like you.

CHAPTER TWO
Reading Group Guide

Should IQ tests be administered in schools? Consider the pros and cons of receiving an IQ score as a child or young person. What is your IQ? How will (has) knowing support(ed) or detract(ed) from your success? If you don't know your IQ score, do you want to know? Why? Why not?

What is the problem with Dr. Terman handpicking subjects for his study or reportedly providing support in their educational pursuits? Should you have considerations before acting upon conclusions from any study? What are some questions you might want to ask the participating scientists?

Shifting Ideas to Action

Consider investigating Dr. Daniel Goleman's work on what he and others have coined *Emotional Intelligence* (EQ). Decide if you would prefer to have a higher IQ or EQ. In your research you'll learn that EQ differs from IQ in that we can improve our EQ, while IQ is reportedly static throughout life. Although you may decide that a high IQ score is most important than EQ, develop a plan to increase your emotional awareness over the next twelve months for more success and fulfillment in your personal and professional life.

CHAPTER THREE
Reading Group Guide

International travel can be expensive and frustrating in the post-9/11 world. Is it worth it? You decide. Since America is sadly ranked sixth overall on Harvard professor Michael Porter's *2014 Social Progress Index*, we might have a good deal to learn from other countries. Brainstorm with others all the ways in which international travel might enrich your life in the following areas: business savvy, consumer awareness, citizenship, general knowledge, artistic expression, spiritual awareness, etc.

Shifting Ideas to Action

Since you've explored why traveling is valuable, yet so expensive, planning is essential. Visit your local bookstore or library and review a variety of travel books. Decide on the next country you want to visit. Know the reasons why and when you want to go. Start a savings account for this specific trip. Make sure your passport will be valid at that time, or renew it. (If you don't have a passport—get one.) Determine the relevant visas, inoculations, baggage limits, etc. for your trip. Make a "dream board" filled with photos of the places you want to visit on this trip. Tell people about your plan. All of this planning will make the trip many times more probable than if you simply daydream, "someday I'd like to see xyz country."

CHAPTER FOUR
Reading Group Guide

In light of your reading in chapter 4, consider how much talent might be lost to the world because the poor have little, or no voice in the arts, education, government, or documentation of history. Develop thorough responses to each of the following statements:

1) Democracy cannot exist without access to quality education.
2) Access to quality education cannot exist without democracy. Critical thinking will be supported by first defining the essence of "democracy" and "quality education."

Shifting Ideas to Action

Many families seek out homeless shelters during holiday seasons and volunteer to prepare and serve holiday meals to the poor. A homeless shelter director in San Diego complained to me once that his staff needs help all year long. Considering the comprehensive support provided to immigrant families (who were precluded by law from living in many areas of Southern California, although their labor was sorely needed), by All Nations in Los Angeles in the 1930s, seek out social welfare programs in your area, especially those whose mission resonates with you. Considering how Helen and Morle Bailey's lives were likely enriched by the thousands of hours spent serving others, consider experiencing the same joy yourself by volunteering at least two hours a month (not just in November and December).

CHAPTER FIVE
Reading Group Guide

In a post-9/11 world many people (especially Americans) complain that "travelling just isn't what it used to be." Security checks and paying extra to check-in luggage are just two examples of "major" annoyances. Compare today's international travel experience with the conditions the Baileys endured to experience other cultures. Reflect on what has really changed—terror threats—travel safety—global access—traveler grit—traveler self-centeredness—traveler patience—traveler sense of entitlement . . .

Shifting Ideas to Action

Helen's PhD 1934 thesis at University of Southern California focused on the anti-narcotic police work of Sir Thomas Wentworth Russell (Russell Pasha 1879–1954) in Egypt on behalf of the League of Nations. (Reportedly in 1929, one of four adult male Egyptians were heroin addicts.) Read about international conferences that were convened as early as 1909 with the purpose of controlling opiate production for nonmedical use.

After you've learned some history of the illicit drug trade, consider the recent explosion of heroin use in the United States as a result of the over production and misuse of pain medications (heroin being a cheaper alternative). Take responsibility and control your family's use of any pain medications. Consider writing to your government representatives regarding regulation of prescription pain medication production, potency, and importation.

CHAPTER SIX
Reading Group Guide

Brainstorm all the considerations people might have about adopting a child. Are these concerns rational or emotional? Make a new list of all the good reasons to adopt a child (these might be personally relevant for the new parent or the child, or more generally for our society).

Consider the character traits present in some people that allow them to test the limits of societal norms, such as the Baileys did by bringing boys and young men of different ethnicities into their white suburban home. Rate yourself from one to ten (ten being the highest) on each. For example, one trait might be "courage." You rate the courage you demonstrate on a daily basis.

Shifting Ideas to Action

Write down a couple of situations, common in your everyday life, when increasing one of the character traits (listed in response to number 2 above) that would lead to a more fulfilling life. Consider what might be necessary to more regularly demonstrate this behavior. Such a meaningful improvement in your life will cost no money, but you'll likely need to change your thinking and act as if your life makes a difference.

Research national Court Appointed Special Advocates (CASA) for Children programs. Learn what it would take for you to qualify to be a CASA volunteer. Consider working toward that qualification over the next few years to prepare yourself to contribute to the life of an at-risk child, and indeed to our society as did Helen and Morle Bailey.

If volunteering as a CASA is not for you, do some different research. Find out how many children are in foster care in your county. Interview someone at the agency that administers fostering and adoptions. See if you can find out the main reasons children are placed in foster care. Locate not-for-profit groups whose mission aligns closely with the roots of the problem in your community. Find out the volunteer requirements for these various agencies. Make a plan to become qualified to help within the next twelve months.

CHAPTER SEVEN
Reading Group Guide

Has there been a Father Coffield or a Helen Miller Bailey in your life? What exactly did they do? Put yourself in their shoes for a moment. Try to explain what you think motivated them to support you in a way that no one else, except perhaps your parents, has done? How can you position yourself to be able to "pay forward" these acts of confidence and kindness?

If you have not experienced such support, write about qualities you would like someone with authority and power to notice about you. Consider exactly what such a person could do today that would be life changing for you. Describe it in detail. In case a Father Coffield or a Doc Bailey never comes along, how do you think you might search out this kind of support on your own?

Shifting Ideas to Action

Indigenous people were likely living in your area thousands of years before the current inhabitants. Seek out this information at your local historical society, library, or university. Learn what lured these people to the area. Was it the climate, abundance of food, natural protection from enemies, etc.? Now make a plan to enjoy these aspects of your surroundings in a similar way. If this is not possible due to polluted waters, endangered wildlife, lack of walking trails, etc., locate environmental or conservation groups in your area. Get involved with these organizations or with your city government and become an advocate for the preservation or restoration of the natural wonders in your area.

CHAPTER EIGHT
Reading Group Guide

Reflect upon how the world has become a smaller place. On the last page of this chapter Helen describes the trip from Obregon, Mexico, to Tucson, Arizona, as being an eighteen-hour endeavor. Today, in eighteen hours we could be half way around the world, in eighteen seconds we could be communicating via SKYPE to anyone in the world. In what ways do you benefit from technology that supports globalization? Are there downsides to globalization? On balance, which "world" would you prefer, the mid-twentieth century or today? Why?

Shifting Ideas to Action

Most people will not travel extensively to one country over a couple of decades such as Helen and Morle Bailey's summers in Mexico. Therefore, in order to make our international trips as safe, enjoyable, and educational as possible, developing cross-cultural skills and attitudes is very important. In their October 2004 *Harvard Business Review* article, "Cultural Intelligence (CQ)," P. Christopher Earley and Elaine Mosakowski describe CQ as an outsider's ability to interpret someone's unfamiliar and ambiguous behavior the same way that a person's compatriots would.

The next time you visit a different country or an area dissimilar from your own, try to observe and consider the many words and behaviors which you might be interpreting differently than those workers or inhabitants. A few examples might help: (1) how important is excellent performance in this culture, (2) what is the assertiveness nature of the people, (3) how much importance is placed on time, (4) are the people expected to express themselves as individuals or as loyal members of a group, (5) what is the degree to which power is distributed in this culture, etc.

CHAPTER NINE
Reading Group Guide

"After I came back from Macchu Picchu, my life seems almost to be divided into before I went to Macchu Picchu and after I came back," summarized one of the great experiences of Doc Bailey's world travels. Although the eight-thousand-foot ascent to the last Inca city may not appeal to everyone, most people experience a kind of transformational moment in their lives—the birth of a child, the death of a parent, meeting their life partner.

Ponder the thought that often these events are unplanned and yet considered the most consequential of our lives. Consider this idea in light of the teachings of the Dali Lama who encourages us to live mindfully in the moment—that past is gone and future not within our control. His Holiness does not suggest we forgo goals and aspirations, but he reminds us to fully experience the here and now.

Shifting Ideas to Action

The relationship between a student and a teacher can be one of the most important and fulfilling in life. By the very nature of their profession, teachers want to serve. Connecting with a like-minded student is a powerful bond. Today, at least in American schools, a good deal interferes. We have helicopter parents hovering over students, rules regarding who initiates communication (for instance many teachers are refrained from emailing or telephone students after a semester's end). Students won't contact teachers or take advantage of office hours for many reasons, not the least of which is the fad of texting precludes participation in any in-depth discussion. Consider contacting a current or past teacher or student. Let them know how their insights or curiosity impacted your life. Ask them to think of you when they need help with something. Kindle the friendship over the years.

CHAPTER TEN
Reading Group Guide

In chapter 10, you read that Dr. Bailey turned $8 into a college scholarship fund which has assisted deserving college-bound students for over fifty years.

In preparation for a meeting with a small group, research psychologist Albert Bandura's concept of self-efficacy, which *Psychology Today*, lists as "one of the most studied topics in psychology." Combine that information with your everyday observations of friends' and family members' behavior and your work group. Consider why some people seem inclined to "think big" when responding to challenges and opportunities. Make a list of reasons why other people don't ever seem to express high expectations or "big dreams."

Although many of her contemporaries describe Helen's interventions on behalf of her students as "Doc's magic," the supernatural was not involved in creating a scholarship fund to help hundreds of students. Make a list of various activities that likely positioned Dr. Bailey to serve her community in such a major way. Now construct a list of activities that might position you to make important contributions to society in the years ahead.

Shifting Ideas to Action

Scholarship funds often result from the desire to "pay it forward." As you plan your future, in addition to what you will need for a comfortable life, how will you create a legacy? Great accomplishments rarely happen by accident; rather, people (not just the super wealthy) set goals for themselves. Consider setting a legacy goal for yourself today. Perhaps you want to give a $500 scholarship to a graduate from your high school within the next two years. You could reach your goal by saving less than seventy-five cents a day. Research shows that to be effective, goals should be challenging, but achievable. Post your goal in a high-visibility spot in your home for a constant reminder of the good deeds you are actively working toward.

CHAPTER ELEVEN
Reading Group Guide

Helen may have been hopeful for the future of the new African nations she visited in 1962. Half a century later, with few exceptions, the people have suffered from corrupt governments, violent conflicts, ethnic unrest, epidemics, and famine, despite decolonization, multiparty political systems, and rich natural resources.

What lessons can be taken from this ravaged continent? Are there responsibilities we have as educated citizens in our own country that are taken for granted? Should a growing divide between the richest and the poorest in any country be a cause for concern among all citizens? Why? Why no

Shifting Ideas to Action

When you meet people from other countries at work, in school, or out with friends, take time to ask about their homelands. (The most interesting people are the most interested.) People who are so busy talking about themselves may find it difficult to establish authentic friendships. Create a file in your computer wherein you log your new acquaintances' contact information. Make every attempt to stay in touch over the months and years. As you read in chapter 11, these contacts could be helpful during international travels.

CHAPTER TWELVE
Reading Group Guide

Recall a lecture, speech, or conversation that you would define as transformative. Many people recite such inspiring moments with preciseness, regardless of how much time has passed. Consider what caused the words to be so powerful. Was there an element of shock, emotion, humor, or anger involved? Do you think the speaker intended for their words to be so meaningful? Have you told them how much the moment meant to you? What can you learn from this experience and the story relayed in chapter 12 that may serve to make you a more impactful communicator?

Shifting Ideas to Action

Consider adopting a significant attitude shift in response to our materialistic culture. Impulse buying often results in emptiness of the spirit and the pocket. Plastic money (credit cards) facilitates impulsive purchases to the point where often no conscious thought exists. For the next thirty days, before any purchase (from an espresso drink or new pair of jeans, from jewelry or a new car) ask a few questions:

What are the values of the company that manufactured this item (or marketed it)? Am I proud to support their cause? Why do I want this? What purpose will it serve? How will my life be improved because I made this purchase? Or, have the marketers made me feel I need to make this purchase to prove something to myself or others?

When my savings account balance remains at its current low level (because I made this purchase) will I feel in control of my financial well-being?

CHAPTER THIRTEEN
Reading Group Guide

Have you ever had a mentor? How do you think Frank Cruz' life would be different if he had not reached out Helen Miller Bailey? Many successful people seek mentors for different aspects of their life. Take a minute to list people from whom you'd love to receive advice and guidance. Consider how it might make someone feel if you asked them to mentor you. Do you think a mentor relationship could be valuable for both parties? If so, why doesn't everyone have at least one mentor?

Shifting Ideas to Action

Consider becoming an expert at something. Expertise is within your control and a great source of increased self-esteem. Once you've identified your topic seek a mentor who can help you find your way to expert status. Once achieved, seek out others with whom you can share your knowledge.

CHAPTER FOURTEEN
Reading Group Guide

In Hitler's Germany leading up to WWII and the Holocaust, propaganda films, cartoons, and posters depicted Jewish people as rats living in the gutters and breeding excessive numbers of offspring. In small groups, discuss the power of words and images used to convey attitudes or opinions. Why should our society be concerned about "haters" hiding behind the anonymity of social media, or the viral capability of social media used as a tool to promote bias, exclusion, and intolerance? How might your concerns impinge upon others' free speech rights?

We hear the word "transparency" quite often. Write down five ways in which it is valuable in a democratic society. As citizens, do we have the responsibility to speak up when we witness injustice? Write about a time you did not speak up against wrongdoing or about a time when you were either the perpetrator or victim of blaming, stereotyping, injustice, or violence. How long will it take before you forget the incident? Why?

Outline a dissenting opinion to the quote from Supreme Court Justice Oliver Wendall Holmes from *Buck v. Bell*. Just as at the time the justice relied on some legal basis or societal or scientific norms to guide his decision, you may want to refer to the United States Bill of Rights and other precedents to help you compose your opinion.

Shifting Ideas to Action

Learn more about the destructive power of propaganda by visiting the Simon Wiesenthal Museum of Tolerance in Los Angeles or New York City; the Holocaust Memorial Museum in Washington DC; or one of several civil rights museums across the country. Read books and articles on prejudice and discrimination, such as offered by the Southern Poverty Law Center. Seek out and read scholarly articles regarding the 1830 Indian Removal Act, the 1882 Chinese Exclusion Act, Executive Order 9066, California Proposition 187, and other legislation.

Education is about change, even transformation. How will (has) learning about the faulty science of eugenics change(d) your thinking, your behavior, and your definition of citizenship? Document your response in a journal to increase the probability of personal growth.

CHAPTER FIFTEEN
Reading Group Guide

Consider the progression that the following human behaviors and thinking are likely to occur: discrimination, hate crimes, stereotyping, developing bias, and prejudiced feelings. While you may not be able to assess the thinking involved with other people, becoming aware of how thoughts can escalate to action can save you from getting caught up in your own or others' misguided emotions.

Business leaders cite emotional balance as a valued trait in their employees. Consider how easy it is to destroy others' confidence and perhaps upset their emotional stability. How difficult it might be to regain trust and respect.

Shifting Ideas to Action

Compare and contrast women's rights in the United States with France and Saudi Arabia. When did women gain the following:

> right to own property, open bank accounts?
> right to divorce?
> right to drive a vehicle?
> right to vote?
> right to hold public office?
> right to attend college?

If you are surprised, share what you learned and consider supporting groups that promote women's rights in your own country or another.

CPSIA information can be obtained at www.ICGtesting.com
Printed in the USA
BVOW05s2301230215

388915BV00003B/5/P